Creative Bible Lessons

With Questions, Answers & Music For Kids

Kim D. Freeman

Creative Bible Lessons with Questions, Answers & Music for Kids

Kim D. Freeman 2025
All rights reserved.

Printed in the United States of America.

Scriptures are from the King James Version of the Bible-public domain.

This author respects copyright laws. Please do not edit, alter, modify, or borrow any portion of this work and take personal ownership. Buyers are welcome to purchase and share with those in their immediate congregations, homes, and groups. Thank you for being mindful of respecting copyright laws.

ISBN: 978-1-80558-739-2 (Paperback)
ISBN: 978-1-80558-740-8 (Hardcover)

Contact information:
Email: kdfwellspring@gmail.com
Website: kimfreemanproductions.com
YouTube Channel: @Kimfreeman306

Author

The purpose of this book is to provide brief Bible lessons from the Scriptures. IT IS NOT A SUBSTITUTE FOR THE BIBLE! Read the Holy Scriptures first, then integrate the Bible lessons into your study time.

My name is Kim D. Freeman, and I am passionately dedicated to sharing the teachings of our Lord and Savior, Jesus Christ, with young hearts and minds. I commend you for choosing this book for your children; your commitment as parents, teachers, and educators is commendable and crucial.

In the face of the pandemic, as churches struggled with decreased attendance and closed doors, I recognized a vital opportunity to create a resource that fills the gap. This book is designed to enhance the educational process of teaching children God's word, especially when regular church services are inaccessible.

Proverbs 22:6 states, "Train up a child in the way he should go; and when he is old, he will not depart from it." It's essential to assess your training tools and measure their effectiveness. Creative Bible Lessons with Questions, Answers, and Music for Kids is your answer. It provides lessons grounded in Scripture, a range of questions about those Scriptures, and direct answers complete with references.

Music plays a critical role in this creative endeavor. I composed original, engaging, easy-to-learn, and catchy music. These songs support Scripture memorization and empower young minds to remain steadfast in the word. After years of teaching this music, children consistently express their desire to sing those songs again!

Time is of the essence. Our children must understand the truth about this world, and that truth resides in God's love. When God offered us Jesus Christ as a gift to atone for our sins, His desire was for no one to perish but for everyone to repent and accept Jesus Christ as their Savior. It is our responsibility to ensure they grasp this profound truth.

Acknowledgments

My Lord and Savior, Jesus Christ

My Husband, Dr. Kelvin Freeman

My First Students (My Children): Kelvin, Kamille, and Kenneth

My Musician, Mr. Walter Sean-Anthony Roberts

Kingdom Kids Choir

Gospel Tabernacle United Holy Church

Northwestern District Children's Workshop

Mark Hockett/Marco Records

Dylan/Musicol Recording

Table of Contents

Covenants Revised Edition 1
   Lesson 1: Adam & The Adamic Covenant 2
   ♪ It's Amazing 7
   Lesson 2: Noah & the Noahic Covenant 8
   ♪ Step of Faith 12
   Lesson 3: Abraham & the Abrahamic Covenant 13
   ♪ I Am a Promise of God 17
   Lesson 4: Moses & the Mosaic Covenant 18
   ♪ Open Our Eyes 22
David & the Davidic Covenant 23
   Lesson 5: Samuel Anoints David 24
   ♪ I Am a Promise of God 28
   Lesson 6: David Worships 29
   ♪ At The Name of Jesus ♪ 33
   Lesson 7: David Defeats Goliath by Faith 34
   ♪ Step of Faith 38
   Lesson 8: Salvation 39
   ♪ Kingdom Kids 42
The Birth of Jesus Christ 43
   Lesson 9: Gabriel Visits Mary 44
   ♪Nothing is Impossible 47
   Lesson 10: Mary Visits Elisabeth 48
   ♪ My Soul Doth Magnify the Lord 51
   Lesson 11: Jesus Christ is Born 52
   ♪This is the Time to Celebrate 55
   Luke 2:1-7 55

Lesson 12: Glory to God	56
♪Music in the Air	59
Luke 2:8-14	59
Open Our Open Eyes Revised Edition	60
Lesson 13: Repent	61
♪ Repent and Be Baptized ♪	65
Lesson 14: Jesus Blesses the Children	66
♪ My Hands Are Out	69
Lesson 15: Be Humble	70
♪ Right-Left ♪	74
Lesson 16: Blind Bartimaeus, the son of Timaeus	75
Mark 10:46-52	75
♪Jesus, I Want To See ♪	79
Miracles Revised Edition	80
Lesson 17: Jesus Heals the Nobleman's Son	81
♪ Surely the Presence of the Lord is in This Place	84
Lesson 18: Jesus Heals the Paralyzed Man	85
♪ Step of Faith	88
Lesson 19: The Woman with the Issue of Blood	89
♪ Just One Touch	93
Lesson 20: A Woman Anoints Jesus	95
♪ Pour the Oil	99
Jesus Christ and the New Covenant	100
Lesson 21: Jesus, The Perfect Sacrifice	101
♪ In The Beginning	106
Lesson 22: The Humility Sandwich (C.H.O.S.E.N)	108
♪ The Way	112

Covenants
Revised Edition

Lesson 1:
Adam & The Adamic Covenant

Genesis Chapters 2 & 3

Genesis 1:1 says, "In the beginning, God created the heaven and the earth. He spoke things into being for six days and rested on the seventh day. Read Genesis Chapter 1 for the details. God planted trees in the Garden of Eden, which were located to the east. God formed man from the dust of the ground. The man cared for the garden. When the man slept, God took a rib from the man and formed a woman.

Genesis 2 identified two trees: the tree of life and the tree of the knowledge of good and evil (Genesis 2:9). God informed the man about His attention toward the trees. Genesis 2:16-17 says, "And the Lord God commanded the man, saying, Of every tree of the garden thou mayest freely eat: But of the tree of the knowledge of good and evil, thou shalt not eat of it: for in the day that thou eatest thereof thou shalt surely die."

The fall of man began when a cunning serpent approached the woman about the forbidden tree one day. The serpent and the woman conversed, debating God's exact words regarding eating from the tree of the knowledge of good and evil. Discussions occur daily, even among Bible scholars, but we must abide by God's word.

Before long, the woman ate from the forbidden tree. She then gave to her husband, and he also ate from the forbidden tree. The man and the woman sinned, and for the first time, they hid from God. They faced the consequences of the Adamic covenant found in Genesis 3:15, which details the serpent's curse, the redemptive work of Christ on the cross, and humanity's sorrow.

God spoke to the serpent. "Serpent, you are cursed above all beasts. You will move on your belly. You will eat dust every day of your life." Genesis 3:15 says, "I will put enmity between thee and the woman, and between thy seed and her seed; it shall bruise thy head, and thou shalt bruise His heel."

God spoke to the woman. Genesis 3:16 says, "Unto the woman he said, I will greatly multiply thy sorrow and thy conception; in sorrow thou shalt bring forth children: and thy desire shall be to thy husband, and he shall rule over thee."

God spoke to Adam. Genesis 3:17 says, "And unto Adam he said, Because thou hast hearkened unto the voice of thy wife, and hast eaten of the tree, of which I commanded thee, saying, Thou shalt not eat of it: cursed is the ground for thy sake, in sorrow shalt thou eat of it all the days of thy life." You will return to the ground. Adam called his wife Eve.

They faced the consequences of disobedience, but God had a plan for redemption. The punishment for sin is death. Adam and Eve were no longer welcome in the Garden of Eden. God placed Cherubim and a flaming sword to guard the tree of life. Corruption continued on the earth until the Bible introduced Noah.

Lesson 1 Questions

1. What was the garden's name that God placed the man and woman to care for?
2. Name two trees located in the garden.
3. Did God give instructions about the trees? What were the instructions?
4. What would happen if the man ate from the forbidden tree?
5. What two people had a conversation about the forbidden tree besides God and the man?
6. Did the two people obey God's words?
7. What is a word to describe the serpent?
8. Did the woman listen to the serpent or God?
9. Did the man listen to the woman or God?
10. What was the curse from God toward the serpent?
11. What was the curse from God toward the woman?
12. What was the curse from God toward the man?
13. What two things protect the tree of life?

Lesson 1 Answers

1. What was the garden's name that God placed the man to care for?
   The Garden of Eden-Genesis 2:8, 15
2. Name two trees located in the garden.
   The tree of life and the tree of the knowledge of good and evil- Genesis 2:9
3. Did God give instructions about the trees? What were the instructions?
   Yes. "And the Lord God commanded the man, saying, Of every tree of the garden thou mayest freely eat: But of the tree of the knowledge of good and evil, thou shalt not eat of it: for in the day that eatest thereof thou shalt surely die."
4. What would happen if the man ate from the forbidden tree?
   "And the Lord God commanded the man, saying, Of every tree of the garden thou mayest freely eat: But of the tree of the knowledge of good and evil, thou shalt not eat of it: for in the day that eatest thereof thou shalt surely die." - Genesis 2:16-17
5. What two people had a conversation about the forbidden tree besides God and the man?
   The serpent and the woman- Genesis 3:1-5
6. Did the two people obey God's words?
   No. Genesis 3:6
7. What is another word to describe the serpent?
   Subtle, crafty, cunning-Genesis 3:1
8. Did the woman listen to the serpent or God?
   The serpent- Genesis 3:6
9. Did the man listen to the woman or God?
   The woman- Genesis 3:6
10. What was the curse from God toward the serpent?

Cursed above all cattle, on his belly, eat dust, enmity with the woman and between his seed and her seed, the woman's seed bruises his head, serpent's seed bruises Jesus' heel Genesis 3:14

11. What was the curse from God toward the woman?
   Greatly multiply sorrow and conception, bring forth children in sorrow, desire will be to thy husband, and husband rules over the woman- Genesis 3:16
12. What was the curse from God toward the man?
   Cursed is the ground for his sake; eat from the ground in sorrow, where there are thorns and thistles, eat the herb of the field, sweat and work, return to the ground - Genesis 3:17-19.
13. What two things protect the tree of life?
   Cherubim and a flaming sword- Genesis 3:24

♫ It's Amazing

Genesis 1 and 2

God made the moon. He made the sun. He made the antelope to run.
A blade of grass can hold the dew. He made the earth for me and you.
But most of all, the amazing of all, it's amazing that my God made me. (Repeat)

It's amazing to me how my God so big can make someone so small like me.
It's amazing! It's amazing to me how my God so big can make someone so small like me. It's amazing to me!

The sky is blue. The grass is green. There are wonders that we have never seen, but they can't compare to the time when God made me. (Repeat)

It's amazing to me how my God so big can make someone so small like me.
It's amazing, oh yes, it is! It's amazing to me how my God so big can make someone so small like me. It's amazing, oh yes, it is!

It's amazing! It's amazing! It's amazing! It's amazing! To me. To me.

Lesson 2:
Noah & the Noahic Covenant

Genesis Chapters 6-9

Sin persisted among the descendants of Adam and Eve, grieving God's heart. God made provisions through Noah. Genesis 6:7-8 says, "And the Lord said, I will destroy man whom I created from the face of the earth; both man, and beast, and the creeping thing, and the fowls of the air, for it repented me that I have made them. But Noah found grace in the eyes of the Lord."

God spoke to Noah when He observed the corrupt nature of the earth. Genesis 6:13 says, "And God said unto Noah, The end of all flesh is come before me; for the earth is filled with violence through them; and, behold, I will destroy them with the earth."

God instructed Noah to build an ark of gopher wood following specific directions. Noah and his family, consisting of eight people, entered the ark along with male and female animals.

No one had ever experienced an ark or rain, but they obeyed God. I am sure that people wondered about the ark. What was an ark? What was its purpose? Why did they have animals in it? In my imagination, people made fun of Noah and his family, but Noah followed God in every detail.

Genesis 6:22 says, "Thus did Noah; according to all that God commanded him, so did he." Genesis 7:16 says, "And they that went in, went in male and female of all flesh, as God commanded him: and the Lord shut him in. The Lord shut the door to the ark, and it rained for 40 days.

After many days, Noah, his family, and the animals left the ark and sacrificed to the Lord. God said, "Noah and sons, be fruitful, and multiply, and replenish the earth" (Genesis 9:1). "This is the token of the covenant which I make between me and you and every living creature that is with you, for perpetual generations" (Genesis: 9:12). When you see a rainbow in the clouds, it is my promise, my covenant that I will not destroy the earth with a flood again (Genesis 9:15).

Every time you see a rainbow in the sky, it reminds you of God's promise to his people: He will not destroy the earth again by a flood. God keeps His promises to us and reminds us of His word so that we can keep our promises to Him. Are you honoring your promise to the Lord? Are you remaining faithful to Him? Are you living for Him in the best way possible?

Lesson 2 Questions

1. What does sin do to God's heart?
2. Did Noah find grace in anyone's eyes?
3. What did God tell Noah to build?
4. What kind of wood did Noah use?
5. How many people were on the ark?
6. Did Noah follow God's commands?
7. Finish the verse: "And they that went in, went in __ and ____ of all flesh. As God commanded him, and the Lord shut him in."
8. How long did it rain?
9. Who did Noah sacrifice to after he left the ark?
10. Who was to replenish the earth?
11. Finish the verse: "This is a token of the ____ which I make between you and every living creature that is with you, for perpetual ____. I will not destroy the earth by a ____ again.
12. Finish the verse: When you see a ____ in the clouds, it is my ____ not to destroy the earth.

Lesson 2 Answers

1. What does sin do to God's heart?
   Sin grieves God's heart- Genesis 6:6
2. Did Noah find grace in anyone's eyes?
   Yes. Noah found grace in the eyes of the Lord- Genesis 6:8
3. What did God tell Noah to build?
   An ark- Genesis 6:14
4. What kind of wood did Noah use?
   Gopher wood- Genesis 6:14
5. How many people were on the ark?
   8- Genesis 6:18, 7:13
6. Did Noah follow God's commands?
   Yes- Genesis 6:22
7. Finish the verse: **"And they that went in, went in two and two of all flesh, male and female- Genesis 6:15-16**
8. How long did it rain?
   40 days- Genesis 6:17
9. Who did Noah sacrifice to after he left the ark?
   The Lord- Genesis 8:20
10. Who was to replenish the earth?
    Noah and his sons -Genesis 9:1, 7
11. Finish the verse: "This is a token of the **covenant,** which I make between you and every living creature that is with you, for perpetual **generations**. I will not destroy the Earth by a **flood** again- Genesis 9:11, 12, 15
12. Finish the verse: "When you see a **rainbow** in the clouds, it is my **promise/covenant** not to destroy the earth"- Genesis 9:16

    When you see a **rainbow** in the clouds, it is my **promise/covenant** not to destroy the earth- Genesis 9:16

♪ Step of Faith

2 Corinthians 5:7 and Philippians 3:14

I'm taking a step of faith. I'm walking with the Lord.
I can't see my way around. I'll put one foot on the ground.
I press toward the mark above. It's full steam ahead.
I'm on my way. I'm moving ahead. I'm moving ahead.

I'm taking a step, a step of faith.
The power of God is my life. I'm moving ahead.
I'm taking a step, a step of faith.
The power of God is my life. I'm moving ahead.

I'm taking a step of faith. I'm walking with the Lord.
I can't see my way around. I'll put one foot on the ground.
I press toward the mark above. It's full steam ahead.
I'm on my way. I'm moving ahead. I'm moving ahead.

The power of God is my life. I'm moving ahead.
I'm taking a step, a step of faith.
The power of God is my life. I'm moving ahead.

Nothing can stop me. Nothing can block me.
I'm on my way now, a step of faith.
Nothing can stop me. Nothing can block me.
I'm on my way now.

The power of God is in my life. I'm moving ahead.
The power of God is in my life. I'm moving ahead.
The power of God is in my life. I'm moving ahead.

Lesson 3: Abraham & the Abrahamic Covenant

Genesis Chapters 12-17

Sin repeated itself after Noah. Abram was a descendant of Noah. God called Abram out of Ur and from his father's house to an unknown land. Abraham followed God in faith. God blessed Abraham with an unconditional promise through the Abrahamic Covenant.

God said, "I will bless your nation; I will bless you. I will bless your name. You will be a blessing. I will bless them that bless you and curse them that curse you. Blessings come through you to other families (Genesis 12:1-3). I will give this land unto your seed (Genesis 12:7)."

How would you feel if God told you to leave your home and go to a new place? I would feel uncomfortable. I would need to find people to help me learn about the new location and wait for God to guide me to the next step. Abram had faith in God's plan.

Abram continued his journey with Sarai, his wife, and Lot, his nephew. Did Abram question God? Abram and Sarai were old, and I am sure Abram wondered about God's promises because he had no children and was 75 years old. God renewed His promise to Abram.

In Genesis 13:14-17, God reminded Abram of the promise. Abram looked up to the north, south, east, and west. "I will make your seed as the dust of the earth, so walk through the land," said God. "Everything is yours." In Genesis 16, Abram and Sarai attempted to help God and hasten the promise of a seed. As a result, Abram had a child with Hagar, another woman.

God spoke again in Genesis 15:1, saying, "Fear not, Abram: I am thy shield and thy exceeding great reward." When Abram reminded

God that he was childless, God said in Genesis 15:4, "This shall not be thine heir; but he that shall come forth out of thine own bowels shall be thine heir."

Genesis 15:6 says, "And he believed in the Lord; and he counted it to him for righteousness."

God spoke to Abram again when he turned 99 years old. God instructed him to walk before Him and be perfect. God emphasized the blessing of his descendants and the promise of the land.

God changed Abram's name to Abraham. He told Abraham that circumcision signified a token of the covenant between them. God changed Sarai's name to Sarah. The Lord blessed them with a child named Isaac when Abraham was 100 and Sarah was 90. (Genesis 17:1-19). Sin continued in the land.

Lesson 3 Questions

1. Who told Abram to leave his father's house?
2. Where was Abram going?
3. Finish the verse: I will bless your n___, I will bless your n___, I will bless y__. I will bless them that ___ you and curse those that ___ you.
4. What was the name of Abram's wife and Abram's nephew?
5. Finish the verse: I will make your ___ as the dust of the earth.
6. Fear not, Abram: I am thy ___ and thy exceeding great ___.
7. He believed God, and he ___ it to him for ____.
8. God changed Abram's name to ___ and Sarai's name to ___.
9. ___ signified a token of the covenant between Abraham and God.
10. What was the name of Abraham's son?

Lesson 3 Answers

1. Who told Abram to leave his father's house?
   The Lord- Genesis 12:1
2. Where was Abram going?
   Unknown-Genesis 12:1
3. Finish the verse: "You will be a great **nation**, I will bless your **name**, I will bless **you**. I will bless them that **bless** you and curse those that **curse** you"- Genesis 12:2-4.
4. What was the name of Abram's wife?
   -Sarai, Sarah, and Lot- Genesis 12:5, 17:15
5. Finish the verse: "I will make your **seed** as the dust of the earth"- Genesis 13:16
6. Finish the verse: "Fear not, Abram, I am thy **shield** and thy exceeding great **reward.**"- Genesis 15:1
7. Finish the verse: "He believed God, and he **counted** it to him for **righteousness.**"- Genesis 15:6
   He believed God, and he **counted** it to him for **righteousness**- Genesis 15:6
8. The Lord changed Abram's name to **Abraham** and Sarai's name to **Sarah**- Genesis 17:5, 15
9. **Circumcision** signified a token of the covenant between Abraham and God- Genesis 17:10-11
10. What was the name of Abraham's son?
    Isaac- Genesis 17:19

♫ I Am a Promise of God

Galatians 3:26-29

God cares about His promises.
God cares. He said in His word.
God cares about His promises.
I am a promise of God.

God cares about His promises.
God cares. He said in His word.
God cares about His promises.
I am a promise of God.

I am an heir, joint heirs with Jesus.
An heir; I am a promise.
An heir; Abraham's seed.
I am a promise of God.

I am an heir, joint heirs with Jesus.
An heir; I am a promise.
An heir; Abraham's seed.
I am a promise of God. Yes, I am a promise of God.

I am, I am a promise. I am, I am a promise of God.
I am, I am a promise. I am, I am a promise of God.
I am, I am a promise. I am, I am a promise of God.
I am, I am a promise.

I am a promise of God. Yes, I am a promise of God.
Yes, I am a promise of God.

Lesson 4:
Moses & the Mosaic Covenant

Exodus 3-20

Exodus 3:1-2 says, "Now Moses kept the flock of his father-in-law the priest of Midian: and he led the flock to the backside of the desert, and came to the mountain of God, even to Horeb. And the angel of the Lord appeared unto him in a flame of fire out of the midst of a bush: and he looked, and, behold, the bush burned with fire, and the bush was not consumed" (Exodus 3:1-2).

Moses looked at the burning bush and then looked away. He said, "I will now turn aside and see this great sight, why the bush is not burnt" (Exodus 3:3). Then the Lord called, "Moses, Moses," and he answered.

The Lord said, "Take off your shoes for you are standing on Holy ground." (Exodus 3:5). Moses took off his shoes. I am the God of Abraham, Isaac, and Jacob. Go to Pharaoh and tell him I want him to let my people go from his bondage. You will lead my people out of Egypt. (Exodus 3:6-10).

Moses asked great questions: Who am I that I should go to Pharaoh? Who shall I say is sending me for such a task? (Exodus 3:11, 13). The Lord had a profound response: "I AM THAT I AM." (Exodus 3:14a). Moses was unsure of what to do. He thought of his faults: Lord, I don't talk very well. How can I go before anyone?

The Lord always has the correct answer. The Lord said, "Aaron, your brother speaks well. You shall speak to Aaron and put words in his mouth; and I will be with your mouth and his mouth and teach you what you shall do" (Exodus 4:14-15).

Even after escaping Egypt, Moses and the Israelites endured the ten plagues, followed the pillars of cloud and fire, crossed the Red Sea and the Jordan River, received manna, and drank water from the rock. However, they forgot God's blessings.

Moses said, "I will go to Mt. Sinai to hear from the Lord." On Mount Sinai, Moses received the Ten Commandments from the Lord. He did this twice and said we must abide by all the Lord says.

God introduced the Mosaic Covenant in Exodus 19:5-8. The covenant included the Ten Commandments, social requirements, and ordinances to reveal sin. This covenant did not save or eliminate sin but directed people to a perfect Savior, the promised seed, the One coming through the line of David. John 1:17 says, "For the law was given by Moses, but grace and truth came by Jesus Christ." Sin continued in the land.

Lesson 4 Questions

1. The angel of the Lord appeared to Moses in a burning ___.
2. The Lord told Moses to take off his ___, for he was standing on ___ ground.
3. Who was Moses going to see to let his people go?
4. Moses asked the Lord: Who shall I say is sending me for the task. What did the Lord say as a response?
5. What was the name of Moses' brother?
6. Moses went to __ ____ to hear from the Lord.
7. How many commandments did Moses receive?

Lesson 4 Answers

1. The angel of the Lord appeared to Moses in a burning **bush**- Exodus 3:2-3
2. The Lord told Moses to take off his **shoes**, for he was standing on **holy** ground- Exodus 3:5
3. Who was Moses going to see to let his people go?
   Pharaoh- Exodus 3:10
4. Moses asked the Lord: Who shall I say is sending me for the task? What did the Lord say as a response?
   I AM THAT I AM-Exodus 3:14
5. What was the name of Moses' brother?
   Aaron- Exodus 4:14
6. Moses went to __ ____ to hear from the Lord.
   Mount Sinai- Exodus 19:1-3
7. How many commandments did Moses receive?
   Ten Commandments- Exodus 20:1-7

♫ Open Our Eyes

Psalm 119:18

Open our eyes to the things before us. Open our eyes to the ways that you move. Open our eyes so that we do not miss you for you are speaking a word in us. (Repeat)

Come into the service. Touch this one and that. Move all through the pews from the front to the back. Anoint us and make us a sight to behold. Open our eyes, Lord. (Repeat)

Open our eyes. Open our eyes. Open our eyes. Open our eyes.
Open our eyes, open our eyes, open our eyes. Open our eyes.
Open our eyes, open our eyes, open our eyes. Open our eyes.

Psalm 119:18 says, Open thou mine eyes, that I behold wondrous things out of thy law.

Open our eyes. Open our eyes. Open my eyes, Father.

David & the Davidic Covenant

Lesson 5:
Samuel Anoints David

I Samuel 16:1-13

David was a shepherd who cared for sheep. He was unaware that a prophet was about to anoint him as king. 1 Samuel 16:1 says, "The Lord said unto Samuel, 'How long will you mourn for Saul, seeing I have rejected him from reigning over Israel? Fill thy horn with oil, and go, I will send thee to Jesse the Bethlehemite: for I have provided me a king among his sons." Samuel felt terrible because he feared Saul, the previous king. When Samuel visited Jesse, he took a heifer for a sacrifice, as he was there to anoint the king of Israel.

When Samuel arrived at Jesse's home, the elders trembled at his sight. When prophets visited, people wondered about the purpose of the prophet's presence: judgment or peace. Samuel stated his intention for the visit, saying, "Peaceably: I am come to sacrifice unto the Lord." (1 Samuel 16:5a) He sanctified Jesse and his sons and called them to the sacrifice.

The first son passed by Samuel. 1 Samuel 16:7 says, "But the Lord said unto Samuel, Look not on his countenance, or on the height of his stature; because I have refused him: for the Lord seeth not as man seeth; for man looketh on the outward appearance, but the Lord looketh on the heart." Jesse's sons passed before Samuel, including Abinadab and Shammah, but God did not choose any of them. Once more, all seven brothers passed before Samuel, yet God did not select them.

Samuel asked Jesse a fundamental question: "Are here all thy children?" (1 Samuel 16:11a)
Jesses stated that the youngest was with the sheep. Samuel did not sit down, so Jesse sent for David, the youngest child. When David arrived, he was ruddy, with a beautiful countenance and good looks. 1

Samuel 16:12b says, "And the Lord said, Arise, anoint him: for this is he."

Samuel took the horn of oil and anointed David among his brothers. 1 Samuel 16:13b says, "and the Spirit of the Lord came upon David from that day forward." God established His kingdom through the line of David. Ruth 4:21-22 says, "And Salmon begat Boaz, and Boaz begat Obed, And Obed begat Jesse, and Jesse begat David."

The Lord conveyed the Davidic Covenant, God's unconditional promise, through Nathan to David. This covenant clarified Jesus Christ's rulership through David's lineage.

2 Samuel 7:4-16 summarizes the David Covenant: "The Lord of hosts says, I took thee from the sheepcote, from following the sheep, to be ruler over my people Israel. The Lord will plant his people. He will make a house. And when your days be fulfilled, and you shall sleep with your fathers, He will set up His seed after you, which shall come out of your bowels. He will establish His kingdom. He will establish his throne forever."

Lesson 5 Questions

1. What question did the Lord ask Samuel?
2. Where did the Lord tell Samuel to go?
3. What was the name of David's dad?
4. The Lord wanted Samuel to anoint a son for what position?
5. The first son passed before Samuel, but what did the Lord say about the appearance of the son?
6. What did the Lord say about all seven sons?
7. Where was David when the seven sons passed before Samuel?
8. Tell me something about David's appearance.
9. What did the Lord tell Samuel to do when David arrived?
10. Who was there when Samuel anointed David?
11. What happened to David after Samuel anointed him?
12. Was David in Jesus' royal bloodline?

Lesson 5 Answers

1. What question did the Lord ask Samuel?
   How long wilt thou mourn for Saul? 1 Samuel 16:1
2. Where did the Lord tell Samuel to go?
   Bethlehem, the house of Jesse- 1 Samuel 16:1, 4
3. What was the name of David's dad?
   Jesse- 1 Samuel 16:1
4. The Lord wanted Samuel to anoint a son for what position?
   King- 1 Samuel 16:1
5. The first son passed before Samuel, but what did the Lord say about the appearance of the son?
   Look not on his countenance, or on the height of his stature: because I have refused him: for the Lord seeth not as man seeth; for man looketh on the outward appearance, but the Lord looketh on the heart-1 Samuel 16:7
6. What did the Lord say about all seven sons?
   The Lord hath not chosen these- 1 Samuel 16:9-10
7. Where was David when the seven sons passed before Samuel?
   Keeping the sheep- 1 Samuel 16:11
8. Tell me something about David's appearance.
   **David was ruddy, he had a beautiful countenance, and he was good-looking-
   1 Samuel 16:12**
9. What did the Lord tell Samuel to do when David arrived?
   Arise, anoint him 1 Samuel 16:12
10. Who was there when Samuel anointed David?
    Jesse and David's brothers- 1 Samuel 16:12-13
11. What happened to David after Samuel anointed him?
    The Spirit of the Lord came upon David from that day forward- 1 Samuel 16:13
12. Was David in Jesus' royal bloodline?
    Yes. Ruth 4:21-22, 2 Samuel 7

♪ I Am a Promise of God

Galatians 3:26-29

God cares about His promises.
God cares. He said in His word.
God cares about His promises.
I am a promise of God.

God cares about His promises.
God cares. He said in His word.
God cares about His promises.
I am a promise of God.

I am an heir, joint heirs with Jesus.
An heir; I am a promise.
An heir; Abraham's seed.
I am a promise of God.

I am an heir, joint heirs with Jesus.
An heir; I am a promise.
An heir; Abraham's seed.
I am a promise of God. Yes, I am a promise of God.

I am, I am a promise. I am, I am a promise of God.
I am, I am a promise. I am, I am a promise of God.
I am, I am a promise. I am, I am a promise of God.
I am, I am a promise.

I am a promise of God. Yes, I am a promise of God.
Yes, I am a promise of God.

Lesson 6:
David Worships

1 Samuel 16:14-23

Children are not too young to worship. Worship is about responding to God's presence and allowing Him His way. David created an atmosphere of worship while tending sheep. He wrote psalms that reflect his relationship with the Lord. David loved the Lord, and the Lord loved David. He brought that same atmosphere of worship while playing the harp before Saul.

Lesson six begins with changes: 1 Samuel 16:14 states, "But the Spirit of the Lord departed from Saul, and an evil spirit from the Lord troubled him." Saul did not fulfill all that the Lord asked of him. The truth is that Saul was deliberately disobedient. The Lord desires our obedience and respect for His ways. There are consequences for disobedience. Romans 6:23 says, "For the wages of sin is death, but the gift of God is eternal life through Christ Jesus our Lord."

Saul's servants noticed a change in him. They recognized that an evil spirit troubled Saul; therefore, they searched for a man who was a skilled harp player. The evil spirit departed when the skillful man played the harp.

Worship creates an opportunity to submit to God. David worshipped before the Lord.

1 Samuel 16:16b says, "and it shall come to pass, when the evil spirit from God is upon thee, that he shall play with his hand, and thou shalt be well." Saul instructed his servants to find this man.

One of the servants spoke and said, "Behold, I have seen a son of Jesse the Bethlehemite, that is cunning in playing; and a mighty valiant man, and a man of war, and prudent in matters, and a comely person, and the Lord is with him (1 Samuel 16:18). I bet that David did not realize that others observed his actions with the sheep in the field or as he played the harp.

David had a new title: Saul's armor-bearer. Before long, David stood before Saul to play the harp, worshipping the Lord in his presence. 1 Samuel 16:23 says, "And it came to pass, when the evil spirit from God was upon Saul, that David took a harp, and played with his hand: so Saul was refreshed and was well, and the evil spirit departed from him." Like David, children worship the Lord when they respond to His presence and allow Him His way.

Lesson 6 Questions

1. Are children too young to worship?
2. Finish the Scripture: But the Spirit of the lord departed from ____ and an evil spirit ____him.
3. Finish the Scripture: For the wages of ___ is ____, but the ___of God is ____ ___ through _____ ____ our Lord. (Romans 6:23)
4. They searched for a man who was a cunning player on the ____.
5. Who knew that David was skillful on the harp?
6. What was David's new title?
7. What happened when an evil spirit was upon Saul?
8. Did Saul get better?
9. What happened to the evil spirit that came from God?

Lesson 6 Answers

1. Are children too young to worship?
   No. 1 Samuel 16:22-23, Matthew 11:25
2. Finish the Scripture: "But the Spirit of the Lord departed from **Saul**, and an evil spirit **troubled** him."-1 Samuel 16:14
3. Finish the Scripture: "For the wages of sin is **death**, but the gift of God is **eternal life** through **Jesus Christ** our Lord."- **Romans 6:23**
4. They searched for a man who was a cunning player on the ____.
   Harp- 1 Samuel 16:16
5. Who knew that David was skillful on the harp?
   One of the servants- 1 Samuel 16:18
6. What was David's new title?
   Saul's armor-bearer- 1 Samuel 16:21
7. What happened when an evil spirit was upon Saul?
   David took a harp, and played with his hand: so Saul was refreshed, and was well, and the evil spirit departed from him- 1 Samuel 16:23
8. Did Saul get better?
   Yes. **David took a harp, and played with his hand: so Saul was refreshed, and was well, and the evil spirit departed from him- 1 Samuel 16:23**
9. What happened to the evil spirit that came from God?
   It departed from Saul- **David took a harp, and played with his hand: so Saul was refreshed, and was well, and the evil spirit departed from him- 1 Samuel 16:23**

♫ At The Name of Jesus ♫

Isaiah 45:23-24; Philippians 2:5-11.

At the name of Jesus, every knee shall bow.
At the name of Jesus, every knee shall bow.
At His name, the enemy trembles.
At His name, sick bodies are healed.
At the name of Jesus, every knee shall bow. Every knee shall bow.

The name of Jesus is holy and precious.
He's more than precious to me.
He is so great, the Son of the Highest.
He rules and reigns as our King.
His name is above every name. All things are under His feet.
Come bow your knees and worship Him. Worship the Holy King at His name.

At the name of Jesus, every knee shall bow.
At the name of Jesus, every knee shall bow.
At His name, the enemy trembles
At His name, sick bodies are healed.
At the name of Jesus, every knee shall bow. Every knee shall bow.

At I'm gonna call on Jesus. At I'm gonna call on Jesus.
At I'm gonna call on Jesus. At I'm gonna call on Jesus.

At I said the enemy trembles. At I said the enemy trembles.
At I said the enemy trembles. At I said the enemy trembles.

At Jesus, Jesus, Jesus. At Jesus, Jesus, Jesus.
At Jesus, Jesus, Jesus. At Jesus, Jesus, Jesus.
At the name of Jesus
Every knee shall bow. Every knee shall bow. Every knee shall bow.

Lesson 7:
David Defeats Goliath by Faith

1 Samuel 17

It was time for war between the Israelites and the Philistines. The Israelites camped on the hill north of the Elah Valley, while the Philistines camped to the south. For 40 days, Goliath challenged anyone to fight him. No one, including King Saul or David's brothers, accepted the challenge. Goliath said in summarizing, "If I win the fight, you will serve us, but if you win, we will serve you." Goliath challenged the Israelites in the morning and evening for 40 days.

Jesse told David to take food to his brothers. When David arrived, he found the Israelites facing a challenge from Goliath of Gath and noticed their fear. David saw a giant who stood six cubits and a span tall. However, David was not afraid of Goliath's size or the challenge because he had faith in the Lord. The winner of the fight received great riches, the king's daughter, and his father's house free in Israel (1 Samuel 17:25).

Four significant events took place before the fight: First, David posed a series of questions, one of which was, "Who is this uncircumcised Philistine, that he should defy the armies of the living God?" (1 Samuel 17:26b) Second, his brothers did not support David in his desire to confront the giant. Third, Saul attempted to offer David his armor, but David replied that "he had not proved them" (1 Samuel 17:39) or tested them and had never fought a battle with someone else's gear. Fourth, David had a staff, five smooth stones, and a sling as weapons.

David approached Goliath. Goliath looked at David as if he were unworthy of the fight, saying, "Am I a dog, that thou cometh to me with staves?" (1 Samuel 17:43). Another word for stave is stick. Goliath cursed David, declaring, "Come to me, and I will give thy flesh unto the fowls of the air, and the beasts of the field" (1 Samuel 17:44).

David was not fearful at all. 1 Samuel 17:45 says, "Then said David to the Philistine, Thou comest to me with a sword, and with a spear, and with a shield: but I come in the name of the Lord of hosts, the God of the armies of Israel, whom thou hast defied." David had much more to say. In summarizing 1 Samuel 17:46-47, David declared, I will kill you and give your body to the fowls of the air and the beasts of the earth. David spoke the truth by faith: the battle is the Lord's.

David took a stone, slung it, and hit Goliath in the forehead. After Goliath fell, David took Goliath's sword and cut his head off. Remember that David killed the lion and the bear in previous verses, so he had practice as a defender. He was not fearful because he knew that God was with him. Children do not have to fear because God is with them as well. God wants us to take steps of faith as we serve Him.

Lesson 7 Questions

1. There was a battle between two groups of people. David was an _____, and Goliath was a _____.
2. What was the challenge of Goliath? If I win the fight, _____. If you win the fight_____.
3. How long did the challenge last?
4. What did the winner receive? ____ _____ _____
5. What did Saul offer David for the fight?
6. What did David do with what Saul offered for the fight?
7. What did David use for the fight?
8. Finish the verse: Am I a dog, that thou comest to me with ___?
9. Finish the verse: But I come in the name of _____
10. How did Goliath die?

Lesson 7 Answers

1. There was a battle between two groups of people. David was an **Israelite,** and Goliath was a **Philistine.** 1 Samuel 17:1-3
2. What was the challenge of Goliath? **If I win the fight, you will serve us. If you win the fight, we will serve you 1 Samuel 17:9**
3. How long did the challenge last? **40 days- 1 Samuel 17:16**
4. What did the winner receive? ____ _____ _____
   Great riches, the king's daughter, and father's house free in Israel- 1 Samuel 17:25
5. What did Saul offer David for the fight? **Saul offered his personal armor, a helmet, and a coat of mail- 1 Samuel 17:38-39**
6. What did David do with what Saul offered for the fight? **David put them off- 1 Samuel 17:39**
7. What did David use for the fight? **A staff, five smooth stones, and a sling- 1 Samuel 17:40**
8. Finish the verse: "Am I a dog, that thou comest to me with **staves/sticks?**"- 1 Samuel 17:43
9. Finish the verse: But I come in the name of **the Lord of hosts, the God of the armies of Israel-** 1 Samuel 17:45
10. How did Goliath die?
    David hit Goliath in the forehead with a stone. David then cut Goliath's head off
    1 Samuel 17:49-51

♫ Step of Faith

2 Corinthians 5:7; Philippians 3:14

I'm taking a step of faith. I'm walking with the Lord.
I can't see my way around. I'll put one foot on the ground.
I press toward the mark above. It's full steam ahead.
I'm on my way. I'm moving ahead. I'm moving ahead.

I'm taking a step, a step of faith.
The power of God is my life. I'm moving ahead.
I'm taking a step, a step of faith.
The power of God is my life. I'm moving ahead.

I'm taking a step of faith. I'm walking with the Lord.
I can't see my way around. I'll put one foot on the ground.
I press toward the mark above. It's full steam ahead.
I'm on my way. I'm moving ahead. I'm moving ahead.

I'm taking a step, a step of faith.
The power of God is my life. I'm moving ahead. I'm taking a step, a step of faith.
The power of God is my life, I'm moving ahead.

Nothing can stop me. Nothing can block me.
I'm on my way now, a step of faith.
Nothing can stop me. Nothing can block me.
I'm on my way now.

The power of God is in my life. I'm moving ahead.
The power of God is in my life. I'm moving ahead.
The power of God is in my life. I'm moving ahead.

Lesson 8: Salvation

John 3:16, Ephesians 2:8-9, Romans 10:9-10

Jesus Christ, the Son of God, is the Savior of the world. He gave is life for us. Therefore, we demonstrate our faith by accepting Jesus Christ as our personal Savior. John 3:16-17 says, "For God so loved the world that He gave His only begotten Son, that whosoever believeth in Him should not perish, but have everlasting life. For God sent not His Son into the world to condemn the world; but that the world through Him might be saved."

We demonstrate faith by believing God raised Jesus Christ from the dead. Jesus Christ took the sin of the world upon His shoulders and died in our place so that we might have the right to eternal life. The aspect of faith is that Jesus Christ sacrificed His life for imperfect people. His love is so great that He freely presents Himself as a ransom for our sins according to grace. Ephesians 2:8-9 says, "For by grace are ye saved through faith: and that not of yourselves: it is a gift of God: Not of works, lest any man should boast."

We verbalize faith by confessing Jesus Christ as personal Savior. Romans 10:9-10 says, "That if thou shalt confess with thy mouth the Lord Jesus, and shalt believe in thine heart that God hath raised him from the dead, thou shalt be saved. For with the heart man believeth unto righteousness; and with the mouth confession is made unto salvation."

If you believe that Jesus Christ is the Son of God, you believe that He died for your sins, and you confess that you are a sinner, and you want Jesus Christ to come into your heart, then you are saved. John 14:6 says, "I am the way, the truth, and the life: no man cometh unto the Father, but by me."

Lesson 8 Questions

1. Jesus Christ is the Savior of the _____.
2. Finish the verse: For ___ so loved the _____, that he gave his only begotten ___, that whosoever believeth in Hi shall not _____ but have everlasting _____.
3. Finish the verse: For God sent not His ___ into the world to ___ the world, but that the ___ through Him might be ___.
4. When Jesus Christ died, we received the right to ___ life.
5. Finish the verse: For by ___ are we saved through ___: and that not of ___: it is a ___ of God: not of ___, lest any man should _____.
6. Finish the verse: That if thou shalt___ with thy ___ the Lord Jesus, and shalt _____ in thine heart that God raised Hom from the ___, thou shalt be _____.
7. Finish the verse: For with the ___ man believeth unto righteousness, and with the ___ confession is made unto ___.

Lesson 8 Answers

1. Jesus Christ is the Savior of the **world**. **John 3:16**
2. Finish the verse: "For **God** so loved the **world**, that He gave His only begotten **Son**, that whosoever believeth in Him shall not **perish** but have everlasting **life**"- **John 3:16**
3. Finish the verse: "For God sent not His **Son** into the world to **condemn** the world, but that the **world** through Him might be **saved."**- **John 3:17**
4. When Jesus Christ died, we received the right to **eternal** life. **John 3:16-17**
5. Finish the verse: "For by **grace** are we saved through **faith**; and that not of **yourselves**: it is the **gift** of God: not of **works**, lest any man should **boast.:**- **Ephesians 2:8-9**
6. Finish the verse: "That if thou shalt **confess** with thy mouth the Lord Jesus, and shalt **believe** in thine heart that God raised Him from the **dead**, thou shalt be **saved."**- **Romans 10:9**
7. Finish the verse: "For with the **heart** man believeth unto righteousness, and with the **mouth** confession is made unto salvation."- **Romans 10:10**

♫ Kingdom Kids

Ephesians 4:7-11

We are kingdom kids, and we're here today to celebrate to celebrate.
We are kingdom kids, and we're here today to celebrate to celebrate.
The measure of the gift. The gift of Jesus. Grace He gave to us.
I have a measure. I will use my gift in the body of Christ.
I will serve the Lord all my life. (Repeat one time)

I will use it to perfect the Saints. I will use it for the ministry.
I will edify the body. I will give the Lord all of me. (Repeat once)
We are kingdom kids, and we're here today to celebrate.

The Birth of Jesus Christ

Lesson 9:
Gabriel Visits Mary

Luke Chapter 1:26-38

[26] "And in the sixth month the angel Gabriel was sent from God unto a city of Galilee, named Nazareth,[27] To a virgin espoused to a man whose name was Joseph, of the house of David; and the virgin's name was Mary.[28] And the angel came in unto her, and said, Hail, thou that art highly favoured, the Lord is with thee: blessed art thou among women.

[29] And when she saw him, she was troubled at his saying, and cast in her mind what manner of salutation this should be.[30] And the angel said unto her, Fear not, Mary: for thou hast found favour with God.[31] And, behold, thou shalt conceive in thy womb, and bring forth a son, and shalt call his name JESUS.

[32] He shall be great, and shall be called the Son of the Highest: and the Lord God shall give unto him the throne of his father David: [33] And he shall reign over the house of Jacob for ever; and of his kingdom there shall be no end.[34] Then said Mary unto the angel, How shall this be, seeing I know not a man?

[35] And the angel answered and said unto her, The Holy Ghost shall come upon thee, and the power of the Highest shall overshadow thee: therefore also that holy thing which shall be born of thee shall be called the Son of God.[36] And, behold, thy cousin Elisabeth, she hath also conceived a son in her old age: and this is the sixth month with her, who was called barren.

[37] For with God nothing shall be impossible.[38] And Mary said, Behold the handmaid of the Lord; be it unto me according to thy word. And the angel departed from her."

Lesson 9 Questions

1. What was the name of the angel that visited Mary?
2. Who was Mary going to marry?
3. The angel called her highly ___.
4. Finish the verse: ___ ___ Mary: for thou hast found favour with ___.
5. Finish the verse: And, behold, thou shalt conceive in thy womb and bring forth a ___, and shalt call his name ___.
6. Finish the verse: He shall be great, and shall be called the Son of the ___: and the Lord God shall give unto him the throne of ___. And His kingdom shall be no ___.
7. What did Mary say to the angel, being that she was a virgin?
8. What did the angel say back to Mary? The ___ ___ shall come upon thee, and the ___ of the Highest shall overshadow thee: therefore that ___ thing which shall be born of thee shall be called the ___ of ___.
9. Who was also going to have a baby besides Mary?
10. How was Mary related to her?
11. Was she younger or older than Mary?
12. Finish the verse: For with ___ nothing shall be ___.

Lesson 9 Answers

1. What was the name of the angel that visited Mary?
Gabriel- Luke 1:26-27
2. Who was Mary going to marry?
Joseph- Luke 1:27
3. The angel called her highly **favoured**. Luke 1:28
4. Finish the verse: "**Fear not** Mary; for thou hast found favour with **God.**"-Luke 1:30
5. Finish the verse: And, behold, thou shalt conceive in thy womb and bring forth a **son**, and shalt call his name **Jesus**- Luke 1:31
6. Finish the verse: He shall be great, and shall be called the Son of the **Highest**: and the Lord God shall give unto him the throne of **His father David**. And His kingdom shall be no **end**- Luke 1:32-33
7. What did Mary say to the angel, being that she was a virgin?
How shall this be, seeing I know not a man?- Luke 1:34
8. What did the angel say back to Mary? The **Holy Ghost** shall come upon thee, and the **power** of the Highest shall overshadow thee: therefore that **holy** thing which shall be born of thee shall be called the **Son of God**- Luke 1:35
9. Who was also going to have a baby besides Mary?
Elisabeth- Luke 1:36
10. How was Mary related to her?
Cousin- Luke 1:36
11. Was she younger or older than Mary?
Older- Luke 1:36
12. Finish the verse: "For with **God** nothing shall be **impossible.**"- Luke 1:37

♫ Nothing is Impossible

St. Luke 1:34-37

With God, dear child, nothing is impossible.
With God, dear child, nothing is impossible.
The Holy Ghost shall come upon thee, and the power of the Highest shall overshadow thee. Just believe me. That Holy One in thee shall be called the Son of God, the Son of God, the Son of God.
(Repeat)

With God, dear child, nothing is impossible. With God, dear child, nothing is impossible.

Lesson 10: Mary Visits Elisabeth

Luke 1:39-56

[39] "And Mary arose in those days, and went into the hill country with haste, into a city of Juda; [40]And entered into the house of Zacharias, and saluted Elisabeth. [41] And it came to pass, that, when Elisabeth heard the salutation of Mary, the babe leaped in her womb; and Elisabeth was filled with the Holy Ghost:

[42] And she spake out with a loud voice, and said, Blessed art thou among women, and blessed is the fruit of thy womb. [43] And whence is this to me, that the mother of my Lord should come to me? [44] For, lo, as soon as the voice of thy salutation sounded in mine ears, the babe leaped in my womb for joy.

[45] And blessed is she that believed: for there shall be a performance of those things which were told her from the Lord. [46] And Mary said, My soul doth magnify the Lord, [47] And my spirit hath rejoiced in God my Saviour.

[48] For he hath regarded the low estate of his handmaiden: for, behold, from henceforth all generations shall call me blessed. [49] For he that is mighty hath done to me great things; and holy is his name. [50] And his mercy is on them that fear him from generation to generation.

[51] He hath shewed strength with his arm; he hath scattered the proud in the imagination of their hearts. [52] He hath put down the mighty from their seats, and exalted them of low degree.[53] He hath filled the hungry with good things; and the rich he hath sent empty away.

[54] He hath helped his servant Israel, in remembrance of his mercy; [55] As he spake to our fathers, to Abraham, and to his seed for ever. [56] And Mary abode with her about three months, and returned to her own house."

Lesson 10 Questions

1. Name the city that Mary went to visit Elisabeth?
2. What happened when Elisabeth heard the salutation of Mary? (The baby ___ in her womb and Elizabeth was filled with the ___ ___/
3. Finish the verse: blessed are thou among ___.
4. Mary was called the mother of my ___.
5. Mary said, My soul doth magnify ___ ___ and my ___ hath rejoiced in God my ___.
6. Finish the verse: All nations shall call me ____. ___ is his name.
7. Finish the verse: And his mercy in on them that fear him from Generation to ___.
8. He hath filled the hungry with ___ things.
9. Finish the verse: As he spoke to our fathers, to ___, and to his seed ___ ___.
10. How long did Mary stay with Elisabeth?

Lesson 10 Answers

1. Name the city that Mary went to visit Elisabeth?
Judah- Luke 1:39
2. What happened when Elisabeth heard the salutation of Mary? (The baby **leaped** in her womb, and Elizabeth was filled with the **Holy Ghost**- Luke 1:41
3. Finish the verse: "Blessed art thou among **women**." **Luke 1:42**
4. Mary was called the mother of my **Lord. Luke 1:43**
5. Mary said, "My soul doth magnify **the Lord** and my **spirit** hath rejoiced in God my **Savior"**- Luke 1:47
6. Finish the verse: All **generations** shall call me **blessed. Holy** is his name- **Luke 1:48-49**
7. Finish the verse: And his mercy is on them that fear him from Generation to **Generation. Luke 1:50.**
8. He hath filled the hungry with **good** things **Luke 1:53**
9. Finish the verse: As he spoke to our fathers, to **Abraham**, and to his seed **forever."- Luke 1:55**.
10. How long did Mary stay with Elisabeth?
Three months- Luke 1:56

♫ My Soul Doth Magnify the Lord

St. Luke 1:46-56

My soul doth magnify the Lord, and my spirit hath rejoiced in God my Savior.
He knows that I am low, but I am blessed and holy is His name.

My soul doth magnify the Lord, and my spirit hath rejoiced in God my Savior.
He knows that I am low, but I am blessed and holy is His name.

He is mighty. Mighty is His name. He has done great, great things for me.
And His mercy is on them that fear Him. Holy, holy is His name. Holy, holy is
His name.

I'm the seed of Abraham. Holy is His name.
I'm the seed of Abraham. Holy is His name.
From generation to generation, holy, holy is His name.
From generation to generation, holy, holy is His name.

Holy, Holy is His name.
Holy, Holy is His name.

Lesson 11:
Jesus Christ is Born

Luke 2:1-7

[1] "And it came to pass in those days, that there went out a decree from Caesar Augustus that all the world should be taxed. [2] (And this taxing was first made when Cyrenius was governor of Syria.) [3] And all went to be taxed, every one into his own city.

[4] And Joseph also went up from Galilee, out of the city of Nazareth, into Judaea, unto the city of David, which is called Bethlehem; (because he was of the house and lineage of David:) [5] To be taxed with Mary his espoused wife, being great with child.

[6] And so it was, that, while they were there, the days were accomplished that she should be delivered. [7] And she brought forth her firstborn son, and wrapped him in swaddling clothes, and laid him in a manger; because there was no room for them in the inn."

Lesson 11 Questions

1. Who declared a decree?
2. All the world was to be ____.
3. This occurred when Cyrenius was governor of ____.
4. Joseph traveled from ___ to the city of ___, which is called ___ because he was of the lineage of ___.
5. What was Joseph's espoused wife's name?
6. She was pregnant or great with ___.
7. Mary delivered the baby. What did she wrap him in?
8. Where did she lay him?
9. There was no room in the ___.

Lesson 11 Answers

1. Who declared a decree?
   Caesar Augustus- Luke 2:1
2. "All the world was to be **taxed**." **Luke 2:1**
3. This occurred when Cyrenius was governor of **Syria**. **Luke 2:24**
4. Joseph traveled from **Galilee** to the **City of David,** which is called **Bethlehem** because he was of the lineage of **David- Luke 2:4.**
5. What was Joseph's espoused wife's name?
   Mary- Luke 2:5
6. She was pregnant or great with **child**- Luke 2:5
7. Mary delivered the baby. What did she wrap him in?
   Swaddling clothes- Luke 2:7
8. Where did she lay him?
   In a manger- Luke 2:7
9. There was no room in the **inn- Luke 2:7**

♫This is the Time to Celebrate

Luke 2:1-7

This is the time to celebrate.
This is the time to celebrate.
This is the time to celebrate Jesus, our king. (Repeat)

We're going to adore for He's wonderful and He is the mighty God.
Bow down before Him as the king of kings. I will give Him my all.
He's Alpha and Omega. He is the first, and He is the very last.
He is my Savior. He is my friend. He has washed me from my past.

This is the time to Hallelujah.
This is the time to celebrate.
This is the time to Hallelujah. Jesus, our king. (Repeat)

Lesson 12: Glory to God

Luke 2:8-20

[8] "And there were in the same country shepherds abiding in the field, keeping watch over their flock by night. [9] And, lo, the angel of the Lord came upon them, and the glory of the Lord shone round about them: and they were sore afraid.

[10] And the angel said unto them, Fear not: for, behold, I bring you good tidings of great joy, which shall be to all people. [11] For unto you is born this day in the city of David a Saviour, which is Christ the Lord.

[12] And this shall be a sign unto you; Ye shall find the babe wrapped in swaddling clothes, lying in a manger. [13] And suddenly there was with the angel a multitude of the heavenly host praising God, and saying, [14] Glory to God in the highest, and on earth peace, good will toward men.

[15] And it came to pass, as the angels were gone away from them into heaven, the shepherds said one to another, Let us now go even unto Bethlehem, and see this thing which is come to pass, which the Lord hath made known unto us.

[16] And they came with haste, and found Mary, and Joseph, and the babe lying in a manger.

[17] And when they had seen it, they made known abroad the saying which was told them concerning this child. [18] And all they that heard it wondered at those things which were told them by the shepherds.

[19] But Mary kept all these things, and pondered them in her heart. [20] And the shepherds returned, glorifying and praising God for all the things that they had heard and seen, as it was told unto them."

Lesson 12 Questions

1. Who was abiding in the field in the country?
2. What were they doing there?
3. Who came upon the people in the field?
4. Finish the verse: The glory of the ___ came upon them, and they were ___.
5. The angel said, Fear__, for behold, I bring you ___ tidings of ___ joy, which shall be to all ___. For unto you is ___ in the city of ___, a ___ which is Christ the ___.
6. Finish the verse: And this shall be a ___ unto you. Ye shall find the Babe ___ in swaddling ___, lying in a ___.
7. Finish the verse: Suddenly, there was with the angel a ___ of heavenly host ___ God, and saying, glory to ___ in the highest, and on earth ---, good will toward ___.
8. Who came with haste to find Mary, Joseph, and the baby?
9. Who pondered things in their heart?
10. Finish the verse: "And the shepherds returned, ___ and ___ God for all things that they had ___ and ___, as it was told unto them."

Lesson 12 Answers

1. Who was abiding in the field in the country?
   Shepherds- Luke 2:8
2. What were they doing there?
   Keeping watch over their flock by night- Luke 2:8
3. Who came upon the people in the field?
   The angel of the Lord- Luke 2:9
4. Finish the verse: The glory of the **Lord** came upon them, and they were **sore afraid**- **Luke 2:9**
5. The angel said, Fear **not**, for behold, I bring you **good** tidings of **great** joy, which shall be to all **people**. For unto you is **born** in the city of **David**, a **Savior** which is Christ the Lord- **Luke 2:10-11**.
6. Finish the verse: And this shall be a **sign** unto you. Ye shall find the Babe **wrapped** in swaddling **clothes**, lying in a **manger**- Luke 2:12
7. Finish the verse: Suddenly, there was with the angel a **multitude** of heavenly host **praising** God, and saying, glory to **God** in the highest, and on earth **peace**, good will toward men- **Luke 2:13**.
8. Who came with haste to find Mary, Joseph, and the baby?
   Shepherds- Luke 2:15-16
9. Who pondered things in their heart?
   Mary- Luke 2:19
10. Finish the verse: "And the shepherds returned, **glorifying** and **praising** God for all things that they had **heard** and **seen**, as it was told unto them." **Luke 2:20**

♫ Music in the Air

Luke 2:8-14

When Jesus was born, there was music in the air.
The angel said fear not. Enjoy the music in the air.
Good tidings of great joy was the music in the air.
Glory in the highest became the music in the air.

I can hear music, music, music in the air.
I can hear angels, angels, angels everywhere.
There was a sign of the promise, a babe in swaddling clothes.
Lying in a manger then they saw the heavenly host.

For unto us a child is born, a Savior Christ the Lord.
For unto us a child is born, a Savior Christ the Lord.
For unto us a child is born, a Savior Christ the Lord.
For unto us a child is born, a Savior Christ the Lord.

For unto us a child is born a Savior Christ the Lord.
Music in the air.

Make a joyful noise unto the LORD, all ye lands. Serve the LORD with gladness: come before his presence with singing. Know ye that the LORD he is God: it is he that hath made us, and not we ourselves; we are his people, and the sheep of his pasture. Enter into his gates with thanksgiving, and into his courts with praise: be thankful unto him, and bless his name. For the LORD is good; his mercy is everlasting; and his truth endureth to all generations.

Amen! Thank you, Lord!

Open Our Open Eyes Revised Edition
Mark Chapters 1-10

Lesson 13: Repent

Mark Chapter 1:1-15

The Gospel of Mark refers to Jesus Christ as the Son of God and introduces the world to John the Baptist. John proclaimed repentance and the good news of Jesus' arrival. He baptized Jesus in the Jordan River. As a messenger, his message was straightforward and twofold: repent and look for the One who is mightier than he. To repent means turning away from sin. John the Baptist informed others that Jesus was on the way.

John the Baptist was dressed in camel's hair. He ate locusts and wild honey. John the Baptist introduced himself in Mark 1:3 by saying, "THE VOICE OF ONE CRYING IN THE WILDERNESS, PREPARE YE THE WAY OF THE LORD, MAKE HIS PATHS STRAIGHT." Repent! I am not worthy to untie the shoes of the one coming after me. Repent! Again, he says, Repent! John preached in Mark 1:7-8, saying, "There cometh one mightier than I after me, the latchet of whose shoes I am not worthy to stoop down and unloose. I indeed have baptized you with water, but He shall baptize you with the Holy Ghost."

Jesus came from Nazareth, and John baptized him in the Jordan River. The Spirit, like a dove, rested on him after the baptism as the heavens opened (Mark 1:10). A voice came from heaven saying, "Thou art my beloved Son, in whom I am well pleased" (Mark 1:11). Jesus soon began his ministry to the world and delivered powerful messages to many people.

We find similar Scriptures in Matthew 3:1-12, Luke 3:2-16, and John 1:19-36, as John the Baptist spoke of Jesus Christ. Read each set of Scriptures to explore how the writers are similar and different in their communication with the reader.

Jesus said, "The time is fulfilled, and the kingdom of God is at hand: repent ye, and believe the gospel (Mark 1:15). The Son of man came to open the eyes of those who are lost. The Son of Man called twelve disciples (Mark 3:14), cast out unclean spirits (Mark 1:25, 26), healed a man with leprosy (Mark 1:41, 42), and healed a paralyzed man (Mark 2:1-12). The Son of Man ate with sinners (Mark 2:15-17), healed on the Sabbath (Mark 3:1-6), taught from parables (Mark 4:1-41), calmed the storm (Mark 4:35-41), raised a little girl from the dead (Mark 5:21-43), fed thousands of people (Mark 6:30-44, Mark 8:1-10), walked on water (Mark 6:45-52), healed a deaf and mute man (Mark 7:31-37), and healed a blind man (Mark 8:22-26). The Son of man came to open the eyes of the blind! The Son of man will be seen by many, suffer many things, be rejected by many, be killed, and after three days, rise again (Mark 8:31). Repent and believe the gospel!

Lesson 13 Questions

1. Who was the messenger and forerunner of Jesus Christ?
2. What two things did John the Baptist eat?
3. What was his message?
4. What did John the Baptist say about Jesus?
5. Where was the location of Jesus' baptism?
6. When did the Spirit appear like a dove?
7. Finish the Scriptures: Repent ye and believe the ____. The Son of man came to open the ____ of those who are lost. The Son of Man ate with ____, healed on the ____, calmed the ____, raised a little girl from the ____, walked on ____, and healed a blind ____.

Lesson 13 Answers

1. Who was the messenger and forerunner of Jesus Christ?
   John the Baptist- Matthew 3:3, Mark 1:1-3, Luke 3:3. John 1:23-27
2. What two things did John the Baptist eat?
   Locust and wild honey- Mark 1:6
3. What was his message?
   Repent and prepare the way of the Lord, and believe the gospel – Mark 1:4-8
4. What did John the Baptist say about Jesus?
   "There cometh one mightier than I after me, the latchet of whose shoes I am not worthy to stoop down and unloose. I indeed baptized you with water, but he shall baptize you with the Holy Ghost"- Mark 1:7-8
5. Where was the location of Jesus' baptism?
   Jordan/Jordan River- Mark 1:9
6. When did the Spirit appear like a dove?
   At Jesus ' baptism- Mark 1:10
7. Finish the Scriptures: Repent ye and believe the **gospel (Mark 1:15)**. The Son of man came to open the **eyes** of those who are lost. The Son of Man ate with **sinners (Mark 2:15-17)**, healed on the **sabbath (Mark 3:1-6)**, calmed the **storm (Mark 4:35-41)**, raised a little girl from the **dead (Mark 6:41-43)**, walked on **water (Mark 1:45-52)**, and healed a blind **man (Mark 10:46-52)**.

♫ Repent and Be Baptized ♫

I've come with a message today. A message of hope to live every day.
Open our open eyes. Repent and be baptized.
The message is simple. The message is right.
Repent and be baptized.

I've come with a message today. A message of hope to live every day.
Open our open eyes. Repent and be baptized.
The message is simple. The message is right.
Repent and be baptized.

I've come with a message today. A message of hope to live every day.
Open our open eyes. Repent and be baptized.
The message is simple. The message is right.
Repent and be baptized.

Open our open eyes. Repent and be baptized.
The message is simple. The message is right.
Repent and be baptized.

Lesson 14:
Jesus Blesses the Children

Mark Chapter 10:13-16

This lesson highlights the value of children and the significance that Jesus Christ places on them. The children approached Jesus Christ, but the disciples rebuked those who brought them to Him.

Consequently, Mark 10:14 says, "But when Jesus saw it, He was much displeased, and said unto them, Suffer the little children to come unto Me. And forbid them not: for of such is the kingdom of God." Another word for suffer is allow. Another word for displeased is angry. Children were very significant to His ministry. He valued their input and presence.

The Bible does not name the specific disciples, but indicates that more than one was involved since the word " disciples " is plural. Jesus was not pleased with the disciples' actions. Jesus stated that the children were welcome to come to Him. Even those who followed Jesus closely had to learn how to treat others correctly.

Mark 10:15 records Jesus' words: "Verily I say unto you, Whosoever shall not receive the kingdom of God as a little child, he shall not enter therein" (Mark 10:14-15). We find similar Scriptures in Matthew 19:14 and Luke 18:16. To conclude the lesson, Jesus took those children into His arms, placed His hands on them, and blessed them.

Point of hope: Children do not have to fear when they desire to approach Jesus Christ in prayer. We pray in Jesus' name. Children's voices should not be silent. Jesus Christ awaits hearing from little ones because He knows each name and voice. A child's faith is good enough to reach Jesus Christ. Children are important and worthy of love.

Lesson 14 Questions

1. Who rebuked those who brought the children to Jesus?
2. Was Jesus happy with those who rebuked those who brought the children?
3. What is another word for displeased?
4. What did Jesus say after He saw it?
5. What is another word for "suffer" in this chapter?
6. Finish the verse: Whosoever shall not receive the kingdom of God as a ____ _____, he shall not enter therein.
7. Finish the verse: He took them up in His ___, put his ___ on them, and ____ them.

Lesson 14 Answers

1. Who rebuked those who brought the children to Jesus?
   The disciples- Mark 10: 13-16
2. Was Jesus happy with those who rebuked those who brought the children?
   No-Mark 10:14
3. What is another word for displeased?
   Angry- Mark 10:14
4. What did Jesus say after He saw it?
   Suffer the little children to come unto me, and forbid them not: for of such is the kingdom of God- Mark 10:14
5. What is another word for "suffer" in this chapter?
   Allow, permit- Mark 10:14
6. Finish the verse: Whosoever shall not receive the kingdom of God as a **little child**, he shall not enter therein- **Mark 10:15**
7. Finish the verse: He took them up in His **arms**, put his **hands** on them, and **blessed** them.

♫ My Hands Are Out

Psalm 90:17

My hands are out. My heart is pure. I came to serve forever more.
No right or left. No left or right. My eyes will be open tonight.

My hands are out. My heart is pure. I came to serve forever more.
No right or left. No left or right. My eyes will be open tonight.

Hallelujah. Hallelujah. Hallelujah. Hallelujah.
Hallelujah. Hallelujah. Hallelujah. Hallelujah.

Our Father, who art in heaven, hallowed be thy name. Thy kingdom come,
They will be done on earth as it is in heaven. Give us this day our daily bread.
And forgive us our trespasses as we forgive those who trespass against us.
And lead us not into temptation, but deliver us from evil.
For thine is the kingdom, and the power, and the glory forever, Amen.

Lesson 15: Be Humble

Mark Chapter 10:35-45

This lesson visualizes the desires of two brothers, James and John, the sons of Zebedee. Even though Jesus called them disciples, they needed to learn humility and maturity in their discipleship. They wished to sit at the right and left of Jesus in glory, representing places of honor. Jesus stated that the most critical position is one of servanthood. There is a cost to attaining the highest honors, and Jesus indicated that the two brothers would experience a glimpse of this cost.

Have you ever desired to receive a gift without contributing to its cost? James and John approached Jesus with their desires, expecting Him to fulfill them by granting them places of honor. Jesus explained that God decides these honors. He posed a series of questions to the brothers. First, He asked them, "Ye know not what ye ask: can ye drink of the cup that I drink of?" He followed with another question: "And be baptized with the baptism that I am baptized with?" (Mark 10:38). Jesus reiterated that God decides places of honor.

Why does this matter to children? According to the word of God from James 4:7, we "Submit yourselves to God. Resist the devil, and he will flee from you." We must submit our desires to the will of God. God created us to be free moral agents with minds that can discover beyond fundamental imagination. However, when we act on our desires outside of the will of God, we function outside of His purpose for our lives. James and John learned from Jesus' example. Additional Scripture references for Mark 10:35-45 include St. Matthew 20:20-28.

As children grow, they learn that humility and serving others bring peace, honor, and respect. Maturity in God creates a pathway to success. James 4:10 says, "Humble yourselves in the sight of the Lord, and He will lift you up. Put God first in your desires, and He gets the glory due to His name.

Lesson 15 Questions

1. How were James and John related?
2. What was the name of their father?
3. Were they uncles, cousins, or disciples of Jesus?
4. What did they want to do in glory?
5. What is the best place to show humility? Left, right, or servanthood
6. Jesus asked them, "Can you ___ of the cup that I ____ of?"
7. Jesus also asked," And can you be _____ with the baptism that I am ____ with?"
8. Who decides places of honor?
9. Did Jesus show us how to be a servant?
10. James 4: 10 says, "_____ yourselves in the sight of the _____ and He will ___ you up."

Lesson 15 Answers

1. How were James and John related?
   Brothers- Mark 10:35
2. What was the name of their father?
   Zebedee- Mark 10:35
3. Were they uncles, cousins, or disciples of Jesus?
   Disciples- Mark 3:13-21
4. What did they want to do in glory?
   Sit in places of honor in glory, right and left of Jesus- Mark 10:37
5. What is the best place to show humility? Left, right, or servanthood
   Servanthood- Mark 10:44
6. Jesus asked them, "Can you **drink** of the cup that I **drink** of?" **Mark 10:38**
7. Jesus also asked," And can you be **baptized** with the baptism that I am **baptized** with?"
   Mark 10:38
8. Who decides places of honor?
   Not Jesus- It shall be given to them for whom it is prepared- **Mark 10:40**
9. Did Jesus show us how to be a servant?
   Yes, "For even the Son of man came not to be ministered unto, but to minister, and to give His life a ransom for many." Mark 10:45
10. James 4: 10 says, "**Humble** yourselves in the sight of the **Lord** and He will **lift** you up."

♫ Right-Left ♫

Mark 10:35-45

When we get to glory, I'll be on the right.
When we get to glory, I'll be on the left.
Right-left, right-left, I so desire on the right or the left. (repeat)

I desire a place of honor. I desire a place for me.
I desire that others will see Jesus honoring me.

When we get to glory, I'll be on the right.
When we get to glory, I'll be on the left.
Right-left, right-left, I so desire on the right or the left.

I desire a place of honor. I desire a place for me.
I desire that others will see Jesus honoring me.

When we get to glory, I'll be on the right.
When we get to glory, I'll be on the left.
Right-left, right-left, I so desire on the right or the left.

Right-left, right-left, I so desire on the right or the left.
Right-left, right-left, I so desire on the right or the left.

Lesson 16: Blind Bartimaeus, the son of Timaeus

Mark 10:46-52

Jesus healed a blind man in Mark 8:22-26. There was another blind man in Mark 10:46-52. When we think about Bartimaeus, we might envision a man holding his money cup, jacket, or cloak. Since he lacked physical eyesight, he relied on other ways to communicate with others, such as his voice. Bartimaeus respected Jesus and demonstrated that respect when he called Jesus the son of David.

The disciples traveled with Jesus from Jerusalem to Jericho. The Bible states that Bartimaeus sat by the roadside begging. Mark 10:47 says, "And when he heard that it was Jesus of Nazareth, he began to cry out, and say, Jesus, thou son of David, have mercy on me."

Many people heard Bartimaeus cry out, and they warned him to hold his peace or be quiet, but he did not listen to them. In fact, Bartimaeus cried out even louder for Jesus to have mercy on him. At one point, "Jesus stood still, and commanded Bartimaeus to be called. And they called the blind man, saying unto him, Be of good comfort, rise, he calleth ye." (Mark 10:49)

Bartimaeus did something amazing in front of all the people. He threw aside his garment and went to Jesus. Remember that Bartimaeus was blind. How did he find Jesus? The Bible does not say how he saw Jesus, but I imagine Bartimaeus felt Jesus' presence and connected spiritually with Him. Sheep know the voice of the shepherd, and they follow closely.

"And Jesus answered and said unto him, What wilt thou that I should do unto thee? The blind man said unto Him, "Lord, that I might receive my sight." (Mark 10:51) Jesus told Bartimaeus to go his way because Bartimaeus' faith made him whole. The exact words were, "Go thy way; Thy faith hath made thee whole" (Mark 10:52a). Immediately, Bartimaeus received sight, and he followed Jesus. We overcome physical barriers with spiritual insight. May we allow the Holy Spirit to remove the obstacles obstructing our spiritual vision. Amen!

Lesson 16 Questions

1. Who traveled with Jesus?
2. Where did they come from, and where did they go?
3. Who was begging at the roadside?
4. What was the title of respect the blind man used to describe Jesus?
5. What did the beggar say?
6. What did Jesus say to the blind man?
7. Jesus said, go thy way: thy_____ has made thee _____.
8. Did Jesus touch the blind man's eyes to heal him?
9. What did the blind man do after he was healed?

Lesson 16 Answers

1. Who traveled with Jesus?
   Disciples and a great number of people- Mark 10:46
2. Where did they go? Jericho- **Mark 10:46**
3. Who was begging at the roadside?
   Blind Bartimaeus, the son of Timaeus- Mark 10:46
4. What was the title of respect the blind man used to describe Jesus?
   Son of David- Mark 10:47
5. What did the beggar say?
   Jesus, thou son of David, have mercy on me- Mark 10:47
6. What did Jesus say or ask the blind man?
   What wilt thou that I should do unto thee?- Mark 10:51
7. Jesus said, go thy way: thy <u>**faith**</u> has made thee whole.- **Mark 10:52**
8. Did Jesus touch the blind man's eyes to heal him?
   No. Mark 10:52
9. What did the blind man do after he was healed?
   He followed Jesus in the way- **Mark 10:52**

♫ Jesus, I Want To See ♫

Mark 10:51

Help me to see which way I should go which way I should go I just do not know. Help me to see which way I should go. Jesus, I want to see. Jesus, I want to see. (Repeat)

I want to see the One who had mercy on me. I want to see the One who will heal me. See the One who will open up my eyes. Jesus, I want to see. Jesus, I want to see.

Help me to see which way I should go which way I should go I just do not know. Help me to see which way I should go. Jesus, I want to see. Jesus, I want to see.

I want to see the One who had mercy on me. I want to see the One who will heal me. See the One who will open up my eyes. Jesus, I want to see. Jesus, I want to see. (Repeat)

Miracles
Revised Edition

Lesson 17: Jesus Heals the Nobleman's Son

John 4:43-54

Miracles and healings occur throughout the Bible. The Book of John features many miracles meant to capture readers' attention. Jesus healed based on faith, according to His word and will, and through a touch. However, He did not touch everyone He healed. Some received healing through faith, some followed Jesus' instructions, and others engaged in unusual acts.

Let us examine how Jesus healed a nobleman's son. Jesus went to Galilee, and a nobleman approached him, saying his son was sick. The man wanted Jesus to come and heal his son. Jesus said, "Except ye see signs and wonders, ye will not believe" (John 4:48). The nobleman then spoke to Jesus, asking him to come before his son died. Jesus said, "Go thy way; thy son liveth" (John 4:50), and the man believed what Jesus said. As the man left, his servants met him and told him the child was alive. The miracle occurred when Jesus spoke the word. As a result, the man and his household believed.

In the Gospel of John, we learn about many miracles. John 20:30-31 says, "And many other signs truly did Jesus in the presence of His disciples, which are not written in this book: But these are written, that ye might believe that Jesus is the Christ, the Son of God; and that believing ye might have life through His name."

Lesson 17 Questions

1. Where did Jesus go to heal someone?
2. Who approached Jesus to ask for healing?
3. Who was sick?
4. What did Jesus say to the man?
5. Finish the verse: except ye see ____ and _____, ye will not believe.
6. Finish the verse: Come before my son_____.
7. What did Jesus say to the nobleman about his son? (Thy son____)
8. Who met the nobleman on the way?
9. What did they say?
10. Who believed?
11. Finish the verses: "And many other____ truly did Jesus in the presence of His ____, which are not written in this ____, But these are ____, that ye might ____ that Jesus is the ____, the Son of ____, and that believing ye might have ____ through His ____.

Lesson 17 Answers

1. Where did Jesus go to heal someone?
   Galilee- John 4:43
2. Who approached Jesus to ask for healing?
   The nobleman- John 4:46
3. Who was sick?
   The nobleman's son- John 4:46
4. What did Jesus say to the man?
   Except ye see signs and wonders, ye will not believe- John 4:8
5. Finish the verse: Come before my son **dies**. John 4:49
6. What did Jesus say to the nobleman about his son? **(Thy son lives/liveth) John 4:50**
7. Who met the nobleman on the way?
   Servants- John 4:51
8. What did they say?
   Thy son lives/liveth- John 4:51
9. Who believed?
   The nobleman and his whole house- John 4:53
10. Finish the verses: "And many other **signs** truly did Jesus in the presence of His **disciples**, which are not written in this **book**, But these are **written**, that ye might **believe** that Jesus is the **Christ**, the Son of **God**, and that believing ye might have **life** through His **name**.
    John 20:30-31

♪ Surely the Presence of the Lord is in This Place

Acts 2:1-4

Surely the presence of the Lord is in this place.
I can feel His mighty power and His grace.
I can hear the brush of angel's wings. I see glory on each face.
Surely the presence of the Lord is in this place.

In the midst of His children, the Lord said He would be.
It doesn't take very many it can be just two or three.
And I feel that same sweet Spirit that I felt oft times before.
Surely, I can say I've been with the Lord.

Surely the presence of the Lord is in this place. I can feel
His mighty power and His grace.
I can hear the brush of angels' wings. I see glory on each face.
Surely the presence of the Lord is in this place.

There's a holy hush around us as God's glory fills this place.
I've touched the hem of His garment I can almost see His face.
And my heart is overflowing with the fullness of His joy.
I know without a doubt that I've been with the Lord.

Surely the presence of the Lord is in this place. I can feel
His mighty power and His grace.
I can hear the brush of angels' wings. I see glory on each face.
Surely the presence of the Lord is in this place.

Lesson 18:
Jesus Heals the Paralyzed Man

John 5:1-16

Lesson 10 took place at a fun location for kids: a pool, which was unusual in Jerusalem because it had five porches. Many sick individuals gathered at the pool, each with various conditions that hindered them from living ordinary lives. They waited for the stirring of the water (John 5:3). John 5:4 says, "For an angel went down at a certain season into the pool, and troubled the water: whosoever then first after the troubling of the water stepped in was made whole of whatsoever disease he had."

A man had been at the pool for 38 years. That is a long time to be at any pool! Jesus saw the man at the pool and asked him a question. Jesus said, "Wilt thou be made whole?" (John 5:6). Another way to ask the same question is, Do you want to be whole? The impotent or paralyzed man explained that he did not have anyone to place him in the pool at the time of the troubled water. He also said that someone else stepped into the water before him. Jesus said, "Rise, take up thy bed, and walk" (John 5:8).

John 5:9 says, "And immediately the man was made whole, and took up his bed, and walked: and on the same day was the sabbath." The Jews wanted to persecute Jesus because He healed on the sabbath day. Jesus loved people and did not conform to the world's ways or sayings. He came to give abundant life. Jesus not only healed the man but also made him whole. The man no longer stayed by the water, waited for another to place him there, or worried that someone else had entered the pool before him.

Lesson 18 Questions

1. Where was the pool located?
2. What was unique about the pool?
3. Why were people at the pool?
4. Who troubled the water?
5. What happened to the first person to enter the pool after the water was troubled?
6. How long was the man at the pool?
7. What question did Jesus ask the impotent man?
8. What two things did the man say to Jesus?
9. What three things did Jesus tell the man to do?
10. What happened to the man after Jesus told him to do three things?
11. Was it okay to heal on the sabbath?
12. Did Jesus care that he healed on the sabbath?

Lesson 18 Answers

1. Where was the pool located?
   Jerusalem- John 5:1
2. What was unique about the pool?
   It had five porches- John 5:2
3. Why were people at the pool?
   They were waiting for the troubling of the water so that they could be healed- John 5:4
4. Who troubled the water?
   An angel- John 5:4
5. What happened to the first person to enter the pool after the water was troubled?
   That person was healed of their disease- John 5:4
6. How long was the man at the pool?
   38 years- John 5:5
7. What question did Jesus ask the impotent man?
   Wilt thou be made whole?- John 5:6
8. What two things did the man say to Jesus?
   I have no one to put me in the water. When I try, someone steps in before me- John 5:7
9. What three things did Jesus tell the man to do?
   Rise, take up thy bed, and walk- John 5:8
10. What happened to the man after Jesus told him to do three things?
    He was made whole- John 5:9
11. Was it okay to heal on the sabbath?
    Yes, but others said no- John 5:20
12. Did Jesus care that he healed on the sabbath?
    No. John 5:14

♫ Step of Faith

2 Corinthians 5:7 and Philippians 3:14

I'm taking a step of faith. I'm walking with the Lord.
I can't see my way around. I'll put one foot on the ground.
I press toward the mark above. It's full steam ahead.
I'm on my way. I'm moving ahead. I'm moving ahead.

I'm taking a step, a step of faith.
The power of God is my life. I'm moving ahead.
I'm taking a step, a step of faith.
The power of God is my life. I'm moving ahead.

I'm taking a step of faith. I'm walking with the Lord.
I can't see my way around. I'll put one foot on the ground.
I press toward the mark above. It's full steam ahead.
I'm on my way. I'm moving ahead. I'm moving ahead.

I'm taking a step, a step of faith.
The power of God is my life. I'm moving ahead.
I'm taking a step, a step of faith.
The power of God is my life. I'm moving ahead.

Nothing can stop me. Nothing can block me.
I'm on my way now, a step of faith.
Nothing can stop me. Nothing can block me.
I'm on my way now.

The power of God is in my life. I'm moving ahead.
The power of God is in my life. I'm moving ahead.
The power of God is in my life. I'm moving ahead.

Lesson 19: The Woman with the Issue of Blood

Matthew 9:20-26, Mark 5:24-34, and Luke 8:42-48

Matthew 9:20-22, Mark 5:24–34, and Luke 8:42–48 recount the story of a woman who suffered from a bleeding issue for twelve years and was healed when she touched what had touched Jesus. This highlights the significance of a miraculous and transformational touch from Jesus to an unnamed and unclean woman.

This woman experienced a blood flow for twelve years. While a woman's flow is a natural part of growth and maturity, this unusual case involved a flow lasting twelve years that disrupted her daily life. We know this from the Gospel of Mark 5:26, in which the writer stated, "And had suffered many things of many physicians, and had spent all that she had, and was nothing bettered, but rather grew worse."

I imagine the woman received uncomfortable looks and felt miserable in public. She risked ridicule and embarrassment from those observing the laws; yet, she did not speak of such things. Instead, she focused on her intention to reach Jesus. The Gospel of Matthew 9:21 says, "For she said within herself, If I may but touch his garment, I shall be whole."

The Gospel of Luke 8:44 says, "Came behind him, and touched the border of his garment: and immediately her issue of blood stanched (stopped)." Each writer records the experience differently, but they all agree that Jesus Christ healed the woman according to her faith.

Kids and adults can exercise their faith and approach Jesus with the same persistence and trust. John 3:16 says, "For God so loved the world, that He gave His only begotten Son, that whosoever believeth in him should not perish, but have everlasting life." He awaits our willingness to come to Him.

Lesson 19 Questions

1. Where can we find three accounts of the woman with the issue of blood?
2. How long did the woman have a flow of blood?
3. Did the physicians help her?
4. How much money did she spend to get better?
5. What part of Jesus' clothes did she touch?
6. Did Jesus touch her to heal her?
7. After she touched Jesus' hem, how long did it take for her healing to occur?
8. Finish: If I may but touch his garment, I shall be _____.
9. Finish the verse: You are healed according to your _____.
10. Fill in the blanks: For ___ so loved the _____ that He gave His only begotten ___ that whosoever believeth in Him shall not ___ but have _____ _____.

Lesson 19 Answers

1. Where can we find three accounts of the woman with the issue of blood?
   Matthew 9:20-26, Mark 5:24-34, and Luke 8:42-48
2. How long did the woman have a flow of blood?
   Twelve years- Mark 5:25
3. Did the physicians help her?
   No. And had suffered many things of many physicians, and had spent all that she had, and was nothing bettered, but rather grew worse- Mark 5:26
4. How much money did she spend to get better?
   All that she had- Mark 5:26
5. What part of Jesus' clothes did she touch?
   Clothes, hem, garment- Mark 5:28
6. Did Jesus touch her to heal her?
   No. She touched something that touched Jesus- Mark 5:28
7. After she touched Jesus' hem, how long did it take for her healing to occur?
   It occurred immediately- Mark 5:29
8. Finish: If I may but touch his garment, I shall be **whole**- **Mark 5:28.**
9. Finish the verse: You are healed according to your **faith**- **Mark 5:34.**
10. Fill in the blanks: For **God** so loved the **world** that He gave His only begotten **Son** that whosoever believeth in Him shall not **perish** but have **everlasting life**. **John 3:16**

♫ Just One Touch

Matthew 9:20-22; Mark 5:25-34; and Luke 8:43-48.

Just one touch from the Master's hand, and I know I'll be made whole. Just one touch from the Master's hand, and I know I'll be made whole. I know I'll be made whole.

Just one touch from the Master's hand, and I know I'll be made whole. Just one touch from the Master's hand, and I know I'll be made whole. I know I'll be made whole.

The Bible tells us about a woman with an issue.
She had an issue for twelve long years.
She knew if she could just get to Jesus.
She would be whole and cry no more tears.
She pressed her way to get to the Master.
She touched his clothes and knew she was healed.
The Master said your faith has healed you. You are whole now go in peace.

Just one touch from the Master's hand, and I know I'll be made whole. Just one touch from the Master's hand, and I know I'll be made whole. I know I'll be made whole.

Gonna press my way to get to the Master.
Gonna press my way through all obstacles.
Gonna press my way. Nothing can stop me.
I know I'll be made whole. I know I'll be made whole.

Just one touch from the Master's hand, and I know I'll be made whole. Just one touch from the Master's hand, and I know I'll be made whole. I know I'll be made whole.

He touched me. The Master touched me.
He touched me. The Master touched me. Now I am whole.
He touched me. The Master touched me.
He touched me. the Master touched me. Now I am whole.
He touched me. The Master touched me.
He touched me. The Master touched me. Now I am whole.
He touched me. The Master touched me.
He touched me. The Master touched me. Now I am whole.

Lesson 20:
A Woman Anoints Jesus

Matthew 26:6-13, Mark 14:3-9, Luke 7:36-50, John 12:1-8

Four writers provide four perspectives on a woman who anoints Jesus Christ. To be anointed means to receive power from God to fulfill one's purpose according to God's will.

Matthew 26:7 says, "There came unto Him a woman having an alabaster box of very precious ointment, and poured it on His head, as he sat at meat."

Mark 14:3 says, "And being in Bethany in the house of Simon the leper, as he sat at meat, there came a woman having an alabaster box of ointment of spikenard very precious; and she brake the box, and poured it on his head."

Luke 7:37-38 says, "And behold, a woman in the city, which was a sinner, when she knew that Jesus sat at meat in the Pharisee's house, brought an alabaster box of ointment, And stood at His feet with tears, and did wipe them with her hair, and anointed them with the ointment."

John 12:3 says, "Then took Mary a pound of ointment of spikenard, very costly, and anointed the feet of Jesus, and wiped His feet with her hair: and the house was filled with the odor of the ointment."

Disciples and others (the Bible does not identify who the others are) disagreed with how the woman anointed Jesus. Many thought that the oil sacrifice was a waste of money. Jesus stated that the woman anointed Him for His burial.

We remember the lady's actions even today. The women sacrificed the most valuable thing they owned, the precious ointment, while Jesus sacrificed the purest thing He had: His life. Jesus defended the woman's actions.

Mark 1:10 says, "And straightway coming up out of the water, he saw the heavens opened, and the Spirit like a dove descending upon Him." Jesus recognized that He needed the anointing of the Holy Spirit to fulfill His purpose on earth, which included living and dying for us.

I wrote a song about Jesus' anointing. A specific part of the song says, "I've been anointed to die for you." I did not find a Scripture that states this word for word, but Jesus said in Luke 4:18a, "THE SPIRIT OF THE LORD IS UPON ME BECAUSE HE HATH ANOINTED ME TO PREACH THE GOSPEL."

Lesson 20 Questions

1. How many writers wrote about a woman who anoints Jesus for His burial?
2. What did the woman use to anoint Jesus?
3. Were the disciples happy about the anointing? Why or why not?
4. Was the anointing oil cheap or costly?
5. Jesus was anointed for his_____.
6. Did Jesus defend the work of the woman?
7. Jesus needed the anointing of the ____ ____ to accomplish His purpose.
8. What is another word for the precious oil?
9. The woman sacrificed, and so did ___.
10. Finish the verse: And the spirit like a ___ descending upon Him.

Lesson 20 Answers

1. How many writers wrote about a woman who anoints Jesus for His burial?

   Four: **Matthew 26:6-13, Mark 14:3-9, Luke 7:36-50, John 12:1-8**

2. What did the woman use to anoint Jesus?
   Oil, perfume, spikenard- Mark 14:3-4

3. Were the disciples happy about the anointing? **No.** Why or why not? **They thought that the woman wasted the oil- Mark 14:4-5**

4. Was the anointing oil cheap or costly?
   Costly, expensive- Mark 14:3-5

5. Jesus was anointed for his **burial**- Mark 14:8.

6. Did Jesus defend the work of the woman?
   Yes. He said that she would be remembered for her work- Mark 14:9

7. Jesus needed the anointing of the **Holy Spirit** to accomplish His purpose- **Luke 4:18**

8. What is another word for the precious oil?
   Ointment, perfume, spikenard- Mark 14:3

9. The woman sacrificed, and so did **Jesus- Mark 14:5**.

10. Finish the verse: And the spirit like a **dove** descending upon Him. **Mark 1:10**

♪ Pour the Oil

Matthew 26:6-13; Mark 14:3-9; Luke 7:36-50; John 12:1-8.

As the woman poured oil, costly oil, she said not a mumbling word.
As she came to Jesus, she poured the oil
From His head down to His feet.
The disciple said woman you wasted the oil.
You wasted it for no cause.
But when Jesus heard them refer to the oil, this is just what He said: I've been anointed to die for you. The woman saw no waste.
She poured from my head to my feet.
The poor you have always but Me as your Savior,
I've been anointed to die for you. I've been anointed to die for you.

As the woman poured oil, costly oil, she said not a mumbling word. As she came to Jesus, she poured the oil
From His head down to His feet.
The disciple said woman you wasted the oil. You wasted it for no cause.
But when Jesus heard them refer to the oil, this is just what He said: I've been anointed to die for you. The woman saw no waste.
She poured from My head to My feet.
The poor you have always but Me as your Savior,
I've been anointed to die for you. I've been anointed to die for you.

Pour the oil, the alabaster oil. Pour the oil, the alabaster oil.
Pour the oil, the alabaster oil. Pour the oil, the alabaster oil.
From my head to my feet Pour, pour it pour it on him, the alabaster oil
From my head to my feet Pour, pour it pour it on him, the alabaster oil
From my head to my feet Pour, pour it pour it on him, the alabaster oil
From my head to my feet Pour, pour it pour it on him, the alabaster oil
From my head to my feet

Jesus Christ and the New Covenant

Lesson 21:
Jesus, The Perfect Sacrifice

Mark Chapters 10-16

Jesus shared details of His betrayal at the hands of people who did not understand His purpose. Mark 10:33-34 says, "Behold, we go up to Jerusalem; and the Son of man shall be delivered unto the chief priests, and unto the scribes; and they shall condemn Him to death, and shall deliver Him to the Gentiles: And they shall mock Him, and shall scourge Him, and shall spit upon Him, and shall kill Him: and the third day He shall rise again."

Remember that James and John desired to sit on Jesus' right and left in glory, but Jesus reminded them that the most incredible place to be is in a position of servanthood. Jesus demonstrated how to be a servant, even when he hung on the cross.

In later days, those in Jerusalem experienced Jesus' grand entrance on a donkey, which fulfilled Old Testament prophecy. Many praised Jesus by saying, "HOSANNA; BLESSED IS HE THAT COMETH IN THE NAME OF THE LORD." (Mark 11:9) Later in his ministry, Jesus said that one of His disciples would betray Him. Still, Jesus remained faithful to His purpose, even in the face of betrayal.

In the Garden of Gethsemane, Jesus prayed to the Father as His disciples (Peter, James, and John) struggled to stay awake. Mark 14:36 says, "And He said, Abba, Father, all things are possible unto thee; take away this cup from me: nevertheless not what I will, but what thou wilt. Jesus submitted to the will of the Father.

Jesus prayed a second time, and the disciples slept a second time. Jesus prayed a third time, and they slept a third time. Jesus stated in Mark 14:41c that "It is enough, the hour is come; behold, the Son of man is betrayed into the hands of sinners."

Many others betrayed Jesus, including Judas Iscariot. Officials presented Jesus before the high priest. One disciple, Simon Peter, denied Jesus three times. Elders, along with the whole council, presented Jesus before Pilate.

The crowd that once praised Jesus shouted to release Barrabas, a robber. They shouted, "Crucify Him! Crucify Him! Crucify Him! Crucify Him!" (Mark 15:13). Jesus died on the cross for the sins of the world. The centurion verbalized the truth by saying, "Truly this man was the Son of God" (Mark 15:39c). They carried Jesus away.

Jesus fulfilled the will of the Father and every prophetic word ever spoken about Him. In three days, He rose from the dead, fulfilling the elements of a perfect sacrifice for humankind's sins. He will return to receive those who have confessed Him as Savior and Lord.

When Jesus returns for the Church, He will fulfill all covenants: the Adamic, Noahic, Mosaic, Davidic, and New Covenants based on His sacrifice for humankind.

In Jeremiah 31, the Lord spoke of a new covenant, not one of laws written on paper, but a law in the inward parts, written on the heart. The Lord opened the gift of grace to all who believe in the sacrificial work of Jesus Christ by faith. Amen. We await His next appearance. Let us celebrate.

Lesson 21 Questions

1. Did Jesus share details about His death?
2. What happened to Jesus before they hung Him on the cross? (They shall __ Him, ___ Him. And ___ on Him.)
3. Jesus rode on a donkey into what place?
4. When Jesus rode on a donkey, many people praised Him by saying: Hosanna; Blessed is he who cometh in the name of ___ ___.
5. When Jesus prayed to the Father in the Garden of Gethsemane, Jesus referred to His Father as ___ ___.
6. Finish the verse: Nevertheless. Not as I ___, but they thy___ be ___.
7. What three disciples slept while Jesus prayed?
8. Which disciple betrayed Jesus?
9. Which disciple denied Jesus three times?
10. Finish the verse: The Son of man is betrayed in the hands of ___.
11. The crowd praised Jesus. They said Hosanna. They later said ____ Him.
12. Who said, "Truly this was the Son of God?"
13. The Lord writes the new covenant on the inward parts, specifically on the ___.
14. Will you go with Jesus when he comes back?

Lesson 21 Answers

1. Did Jesus share details about His death?
   Yes: Mark 10:33-34 "Behold, we go up to Jerusalem; and the Son of man shall be delivered unto the chief priests, and unto the scribes; and they shall condemn Him to death, and shall deliver Him to the Gentiles: And they shall mock Him, and shall spit upon Him, and shall kill Him: and the third day rise again."
2. What happened to Jesus before they hung Him on the cross? (They shall **condemn** Him, **mock** Him. And **spit** on Him.) **Mark 10:34**
3. Jesus rode on a donkey into what place?
   Jerusalem- Mark 10:1
4. When Jesus rode on a donkey, many people praised Him by saying: Hosanna; Blessed is he who cometh in the name of **the Lord**. Mark 11:9
5. When Jesus prayed to the Father in the Garden of Gethsemane, Jesus referred to His Father as **Abba Father**. Mark 14:36
6. Finish the verse: Nevertheless. Not what I will, but what thou wilt **(Thy will be done)**
   Mark 14:36.
7. What three disciples slept while Jesus prayed?
   Peter, James, and John- Mark 14:33
8. Which disciple betrayed Jesus for money?
   Judas Iscariot- Mark 14:43-44
9. Which disciple denied Jesus three times?
   Peter- Mark 14:29-30
10. Finish the verse: The Son of man is betrayed in the hands of **sinners**- Mark 14:41.
11. The crowd praised Jesus. They said Hosanna. They later said **Crucify** Him **Mark 15:14.**
12. Who said, "Truly this was the Son of God?"

The Centurion- Mark 15:39

13. The Lord writes the new covenant on the inward parts, specifically on the **mind/<u>heart</u>**- **Jeremiah 31:33**

14. Will you go with Jesus when he comes back?
    Yes. John 3:16

♫ In The Beginning

John 1:1-14, Psalm 119:105.

In the beginning, was the Word. And the Word was with God, and the Word was God. The word began with God. The word started with God. (Repeat)

I said the word; the word will light my day.
I said the word; the word will make a way.
I said the word; the word will save my soul.
I said the word; the word will make me whole.

In the beginning, was the Word.
And the Word was with God, and the Word was God.
The word began with God. The word began with God.

I said the word; the word will light my day.
I said the word; the word will make a way.
I said the word; the word will save my soul.
I said the word; the word will make me whole.

Thy word is a lamp unto my feet; thy word is a light unto my path.
Thy word is a lamp unto my feet; thy word is a light unto my path.
Thy word is a lamp unto my feet; thy word is a light unto my path.
Thy word is a lamp unto my feet, thy word thy word, thy word.

I said the word; the word will light my day.
I said the word; the word will make a way.
I said the word; the word will save my soul.
I said the word; the word will make me whole.

In the beginning, was the Word.
And the Word was with God, and the Word was God.
The word began with God. The word began with God.

Lesson 22: The Humility Sandwich (C.H.O.S.E.N)

Philippians 2:5-11, Hebrews 9:22

There are passages in the Bible that may be difficult for children to understand. Therefore, this writing uses six letters to create a spiritual sandwich that refers to the humility of Jesus Christ from Philippians 2:5-11 and Hebrews 9:22. The recipe book is the Bible. Humility encourages us to live like Jesus Christ.

The first ingredient for our spiritual sandwich is **C,** which stands for Christ. Philippians 2:5-6 says, "Let this mind be in you which was also in Christ Jesus: Who, being in the form of God, thought it not robbery to be equal with God." We should think like Jesus Christ by rejecting negative thoughts.

H is the next ingredient, which stands for Himself. Philippians 2:7 says, "But made Himself of no reputation, and took upon Him the form of a servant, and was made in the likeness of man." Jesus was both God and man simultaneously, and He did not sin. He served as our example of how to serve others.

O, the third ingredient, represents Christ's obedience. Philippians 2:8 says, "And being found in fashion as a man, He humbled Himself, and became obedient unto death, even the death of the cross." He submitted His own will to God the Father and died for the world's sins. He rose on the third day with all power.

S stands for sacrifice. Hebrews 9:22 says, "And almost all things are by the law purged with blood; and without shedding of blood is no remission." Jesus shed His blood for us, which paid for our sin. Jesus took our place on the cross. When we accept Him as our Savior, we receive the promise of eternal life.

E, the fifth letter, stands for exalt. Philippians 2:9 says, "Wherefore, God hath exalted Him, and given Him a name which is above every name." Exalt means to place in the highest honor. No other name compares to the name of Jesus. No other name can save a person from sin. No other name surpasses the name of Jesus.

N, the final letter, represents the name. Philippians 2:10-11 says, "That at the name of Jesus, every knee should bow, of things in heaven, and things in earth, and things under the earth: And that every tongue should confess that Jesus Christ is Lord to the glory of God the Father." Call upon His name and declare Him as your Savior and Lord.

Romans 10:9 says, "That if thou shalt confess with thy mouth the Lord Jesus, and believe that God hath raised Him from the dead, thou shalt be saved." Romans 10:13 says, "FOR WHOSOEVER SHALL CALL UPON THE NAME OF THE LORD SHALL BE SAVED."

Take the humility agreement: Making the humility sandwich requires me to work with others. I will share Jesus Christ's humility daily and be humble in all I do. I will love others and give my heart to Jesus Christ. I will confess Jesus Christ as my Savior and ask Him to forgive my sins. Please come into my heart and help me live for Jesus Christ.

Lesson 22 Questions

1. What does C stand for?
2. Finish the verses: Let this mind be in you which was also in ____ _____: Who, being in the form of ___, thought it not robbery to be ___ with ___:
3. What does H stand for?
4. Finish the verse: But made_____ of no reputation: and took upon Him the form of a _____, and was made in the likeness of ___.
5. What does O stand for?
6. Finish the verse: And being found in fashion as a man, He humbles Himself and became ____ unto death, even the death of the _____.
7. What does S stand for?
8. Finish the verse: And almost all things are by the law purged with blood, and without the ___ of blood is no remission.
9. What does E stand for?
10. Finish the verse: Wherefore, God hath highly _____Him, and given Him a name which is above every name.
11. What does N stand for?
12. Finish the verses: That at the ____ of Jesus, every knee should bow, of things in heaven, and things in earth, and things under the earth. And that every tongue should _____ that ____ ____ is Lord, to the glory of ___ the Father.

Lesson 22 Answers

1. What does C stand for?
   Christ- Philippians 2:5
2. Finish the verses: Let this mind be in you which was also in **Christ Jesus**: Who, being in the form of **God**, thought it not robbery to be **equal** with **God**: Philippians 2:5-6
3. What does H stand for?
   Himself- Philippians 2:7
4. Finish the verse: But made **Himself** of no reputation: and took upon Him the form of a **servant**, and was made in the likeness of **men**. Philippians 2:7
5. What does O stand for?
   Obedient- Philippians 2:8
6. Finish the verse: And being found in fashion as a man, He humbles Himself and became **obedient** unto death, even the death of the **cross**. Philippians 2:8
7. What does S stand for?
   Shedding- Hebrews 9:22
8. Finish the verse: And almost all things are by the law purged with blood, and without the **shedding** of blood is no remission. **Hebrews 9:22**
9. What does E stand for?
   Exalted- Philippians 2:9
10. Finish the verse: Wherefore, God hath highly **exalted** Him, and given Him a name which is above every name. Philippians 2:9
11. What does N stand for?
    Name- Philippians 2:10
12. Finish the verses: That at the **name** of Jesus, every knee should bow, of things in heaven, and things in earth, and things under the earth. And that every tongue should **confess** that **Jesus Christ** is Lord, to the glory of **God** the Father. Philippians 2:10-11

♪ The Way

John 14:6

He is the way, the truth, the life, the way.
He is the way, the truth, the life, the way.
He is the way, the truth, the life, the way.
He is the way, the truth, the life, the way.
He is the way, the truth, the life, the way.
He is the way, the truth, the life, the way.
He is the way, the truth, the life, the way.
He is the way, the truth, the life, the way.

St. John 14:1-6 (KJV)
Let not your heart be troubled: ye believe in God, believe also in me. In my Father's house are many mansions: if it were not so, I would have told you. I go to prepare a place for you. And if I go and prepare a place for you, I will come again, and receive you unto myself; that where I am, there ye may be also. And whither I go ye know, and the way ye know. Thomas saith unto him, Lord, we know not whither thou goest; and how can we know the way? Jesus saith unto him, I am the way, the truth, and the life: no man cometh unto the Father, but by me.